Microsoft® Office Excel® 2016: Part 3

Microsoft® Office Excel® 2016: Part 3

Part Number: 091057
Course Edition: 1.3

Acknowledgements

PROJECT TEAM

Author	Media Designer	Content Editor
William Kelly	Brian Sullivan	Michelle Farney

Logical Operations wishes to thank the Logical Operations Instructor Community, and in particular Gary Leenhouts and Elizabeth Robinson, for their instructional and technical expertise during the creation of this course.

Notices

DISCLAIMER

While Logical Operations, Inc. takes care to ensure the accuracy and quality of these materials, we cannot guarantee their accuracy, and all materials are provided without any warranty whatsoever, including, but not limited to, the implied warranties of merchantability or fitness for a particular purpose. The name used in the data files for this course is that of a fictitious company. Any resemblance to current or future companies is purely coincidental. We do not believe we have used anyone's name in creating this course, but if we have, please notify us and we will change the name in the next revision of the course. Logical Operations is an independent provider of integrated training solutions for individuals, businesses, educational institutions, and government agencies. The use of screenshots, photographs of another entity's products, or another entity's product name or service in this book is for editorial purposes only. No such use should be construed to imply sponsorship or endorsement of the book by nor any affiliation of such entity with Logical Operations. This courseware may contain links to sites on the Internet that are owned and operated by third parties (the "External Sites"). Logical Operations is not responsible for the availability of, or the content located on or through, any External Site. Please contact Logical Operations if you have any concerns regarding such links or External Sites.

TRADEMARK NOTICES

Microsoft® Office Excel® 2016: Part 3

About This Course

Clearly, you use Excel a lot in your role. Otherwise, you wouldn't be taking this course. By now, you're already familiar with Excel 2016, its functions and formulas, a lot of its features and functionality, and its powerful data analysis tools. You are likely called upon to analyze and report on data frequently, work in collaboration with others to deliver actionable organizational intelligence, and keep and maintain workbooks for all manner of purposes. At this level of use and collaboration, you have also likely encountered your fair share of issues and challenges. You're too busy, though, to waste time scouring over workbooks to resolve issues or to perform repetitive, monotonous tasks. You need to know how to get Excel to do more for you so you can focus on what's really important: staying ahead of the competition. That's exactly what this course aims to help you do.

This course builds off of the foundational and intermediate knowledge presented in the *Microsoft® Office Excel® 2016: Part 1* and *Part 2* courses to help you get the most of your Excel experience. The ability to collaborate with colleagues, automate complex or repetitive tasks, and use conditional logic to construct and apply elaborate formulas and functions will put the full power of Excel right at your fingertips. The more you learn about how to get Excel to do the hard work for you, the more you'll be able to focus on getting the answers you need from the vast amounts of data your organization generates.

This course covers Microsoft Office Specialist exam objectives to help students prepare for the Excel 2016 Exam and the Excel 2016 Expert Exam.

Course Description

Target Student

This course is intended for students who are experienced Excel 2016 users and have a desire or need to advance their skills in working with some of the more advanced Excel features. Students will likely need to troubleshoot large, complex workbooks, automate repetitive tasks, engage in collaborative partnerships involving workbook data, construct complex Excel functions, and use those functions to perform rigorous analysis of extensive, complex datasets.

Course Prerequisites

To ensure success, students should have practical, real-world experience creating and analyzing datasets using Excel 2016. Specific tasks students should be able to perform include: creating formulas and using Excel functions; creating, sorting, and filtering datasets and tables; presenting data by using basic charts; creating and working with PivotTables, slicers, and PivotCharts; and customizing the Excel environment. To meet these prerequisites, students can take the following Logical Operations courses, or should possess the equivalent skill level:

- *Microsoft® Office Excel® 2016: Part 1*

- *Microsoft® Office Excel® 2016: Part 2*

Course Objectives

Upon successful completion of this course, you will be able to perform advanced data analysis, collaborate on workbooks with other users, and automate workbook functionality.

You will:

- Work with multiple worksheets and workbooks.
- Use Lookup functions and formula auditing
- Share and protect workbooks.
- Automate workbook functionality.
- Create sparklines and map data.
- Forecast data.

The CHOICE Home Screen

Logon and access information for your CHOICE environment will be provided with your class experience. The CHOICE platform is your entry point to the CHOICE learning experience, of which this course manual is only one part.

On the CHOICE Home screen, you can access the CHOICE Course screens for your specific courses. Visit the CHOICE Course screen both during and after class to make use of the world of support and instructional resources that make up the CHOICE experience.

Each CHOICE Course screen will give you access to the following resources:

- **Classroom**: A link to your training provider's classroom environment.
- **eBook**: An interactive electronic version of the printed book for your course.
- **Files**: Any course files available to download.
- **Checklists**: Step-by-step procedures and general guidelines you can use as a reference during and after class.
- **LearnTOs**: Brief animated videos that enhance and extend the classroom learning experience.
- **Assessment**: A course assessment for your self-assessment of the course content.
- Social media resources that enable you to collaborate with others in the learning community using professional communications sites such as LinkedIn or microblogging tools such as Twitter.

Depending on the nature of your course and the components chosen by your learning provider, the CHOICE Course screen may also include access to elements such as:

- LogicalLABS, a virtual technical environment for your course.
- Various partner resources related to the courseware.
- Related certifications or credentials.
- A link to your training provider's website.
- Notices from the CHOICE administrator.
- Newsletters and other communications from your learning provider.
- Mentoring services.

Visit your CHOICE Home screen often to connect, communicate, and extend your learning experience!

How to Use This Book

As You Learn

This book is divided into lessons and topics, covering a subject or a set of related subjects. In most cases, lessons are arranged in order of increasing proficiency.

The results-oriented topics include relevant and supporting information you need to master the content. Each topic has various types of activities designed to enable you to solidify your understanding of the informational material presented in the course. Information is provided for reference and reflection to facilitate understanding and practice.

Data files for various activities as well as other supporting files for the course are available by download from the CHOICE Course screen. In addition to sample data for the course exercises, the course files may contain media components to enhance your learning and additional reference materials for use both during and after the course.

Checklists of procedures and guidelines can be used during class and as after-class references when you're back on the job and need to refresh your understanding.

At the back of the book, you will find a glossary of the definitions of the terms and concepts used throughout the course. You will also find an index to assist in locating information within the instructional components of the book.

As You Review

Any method of instruction is only as effective as the time and effort you, the student, are willing to invest in it. In addition, some of the information that you learn in class may not be important to you immediately, but it may become important later. For this reason, we encourage you to spend some time reviewing the content of the course after your time in the classroom.

As a Reference

The organization and layout of this book make it an easy-to-use resource for future reference. Taking advantage of the glossary, index, and table of contents, you can use this book as a first source of definitions, background information, and summaries.

Course Icons

Watch throughout the material for the following visual cues.

Icon	Description
	A **Note** provides additional information, guidance, or hints about a topic or task.
	A **Caution** note makes you aware of places where you need to be particularly careful with your actions, settings, or decisions so that you can be sure to get the desired results of an activity or task.
	LearnTO notes show you where an associated LearnTO is particularly relevant to the content. Access LearnTOs from your CHOICE Course screen.
	Checklists provide job aids you can use after class as a reference to perform skills back on the job. Access checklists from your CHOICE Course screen.
	Social notes remind you to check your CHOICE Course screen for opportunities to interact with the CHOICE community using social media.

1 | Working with Multiple Worksheets and Workbooks

Lesson Time: 1 hour

Lesson Introduction

In many cases, you are collecting or tracking data in one or more worksheets in a workbook. While you know how to summarize the data on one worksheet, you may wish to combine the data into a report from these individual worksheets or even from other workbooks. Excel has several features that allow you to aggregate the data to generate those reports.

Using multiple worksheets and workbooks to track, retrieve, consolidate, and report on data can all be done in Microsoft® Excel® 2016. Whether you are using formulas, 3-D formulas and functions, links to external data (meaning other worksheets or workbooks), or consolidating data from identical worksheets, Excel has the tools to do the job.

Lesson Objectives

In this lesson, you will work with multiple worksheets and workbooks. You will:

- Use links and external references.
- Use 3-D references.
- Consolidate data.

TOPIC A

Use Links and External References

As you've likely already discovered, introducing errors in large, complex worksheets can quickly leave you with a mess on your hands. Referring to data in its original location is often better than making copies of the data and then having to update multiple copies when values change. Doing so can introduce errors in your calculations. Fortunately, Excel 2016 enables you to create formulas and functions that link data from multiple worksheets and workbooks in order to create a worksheet or workbook summary, all the while allowing you to maintain and view your original data.

Linked Cells

Excel 2016 provides you with the ability to connect one cell to the data entered into another cell. When you create this connection, you create a *linked cell*. Unlike a cell reference, which merely calls the value in another cell for use in a formula or function, a linked cell behaves as if it actually contains the data in the original cell. If you update the value in the original cell, Excel updates the value in the linked cell automatically. And, as the linked cell behaves as if it actually contains the data in the original cell, you can perform any calculation on the linked cells as you would on the original cell. This allows you to take full advantage of all of Excel's calculation and data analysis functionality without having to worry about introducing errors into your raw data. And, as the linked cells update automatically, so will your calculations.

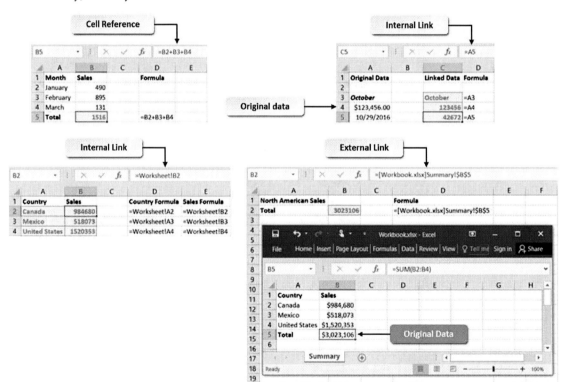

Figure 1-1: Although a linked cell behaves as if it contains the data in the original cell, it actually contains a link to that data.

Note: Links do not include the formatting applied to the original cell.

You can link worksheet cells to cells on the same worksheet as well as other worksheets in the same workbook, or you can link them to cells on worksheets in other workbooks. Links to other worksheets in the same workbook are known as *internal links*. Links to other workbooks are called *external links*. By default, Excel creates graphically selected externally links as absolute references and graphically selected internal links as relative references.

> **Note:** To explore how to add other types of external content to your worksheets, access the **Add Supplemental Information to Worksheets by Embedding Objects** presentation from the **LearnTO** tile on the CHOICE Course screen.

Linked Cell Syntax

You create links to other cells in much the same way you enter a formula into a cell. In fact, you can think of links as a type of specialized formula. As such, with an understanding of the syntax used to create links, you can link a cell to any other cell in its workbook or in another workbook. And, you can take advantage of Excel's AutoFill feature to quickly link entire ranges of data to other ranges. If you use the AutoFill feature to create links, remember that relative and absolute references behave the same way in links as they do in formulas and functions. Typically, you will use only relative references when linking entire ranges of data.

To create an internal link, simply type an equal sign (=) into a cell as if you were typing a formula, enter the desired cell reference, and press **Enter**. If you are linking to a cell on another worksheet, include the worksheet name followed by an exclamation point (!) before the cell reference.

> **Note:** Once you have typed the equal sign, you can also simply select the cell you wish to link to manually. This is the same as entering a reference in a formula or a function.

To create an external link, you will also have to include a pointer to the workbook that contains the cell you are linking to. To do this, simply enter the name of the workbook enclosed in square brackets ([ ]) before the worksheet and cell references. If the workbook containing the data you're linking to is open, you can simply enter the equal sign, switch to the other workbook, select the desired cell, and press **Enter**. When you use the manual-selection method to add an external link, Excel creates the link using absolute references.

The Edit Links Dialog Box

You can use the **Edit Links** dialog box to manage the external links in your Excel workbooks. The **Edit Links** dialog box displays a list of all workbooks that the current workbook has links to. You can access the **Edit Links** dialog box by selecting **Data→Connections→Edit Links**; the **Edit Links** command appears grayed-out if there are no external links in the current workbook.

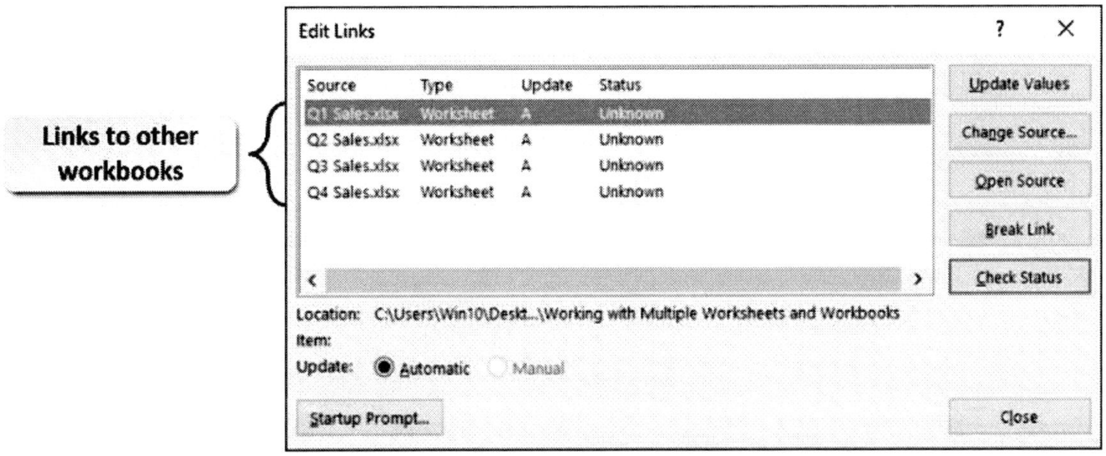

Figure 1-2: Use the Edit Links dialog box to manage external links.

The following table describes the functions of some of the elements of the **Edit Links** dialog box.

Edit Links Dialog Box Element	Description
Update Values button	Updates the values in linked cells if changes have been made to the source data and automatic updates are disabled.
Change Source button	Opens the **Change Source** dialog box, enabling you to change which workbook the current workbook is linked to. You can change links to each external workbook separately.
Open Source button	Opens the workbook you have selected in the **Edit Links** dialog box.
Break Link button	Removes all links to the workbook you have selected in the **Edit Links** dialog box. Once you break the link to a workbook, Excel converts the data in all cells linked to that workbook to constant values.
Check Status button	Displays the status of all external links. This could, for example, let you know if you need to update values or if the source workbook is currently open.
Startup Prompt button	Opens the **Startup Prompt** dialog box, which enables you to determine whether or not Excel displays a warning message when you open workbooks containing links and how you want Excel to treat those links.

External References in Formulas and Functions

Much as you can link cells to other worksheets and external workbooks, you can also use references to cells or ranges on other worksheets or in other workbooks to link Excel formulas and functions to those cells. This enables you to display calculation or function results in a different location than where the raw data is stored. In this way, you don't have to create a linked copy of the dataset range if you don't want to. References to cells or ranges in other workbooks are called *external references*.

The syntax for including references to cells or ranges on other worksheets or in other workbooks is the same as it is for creating links. Whenever you need to include a reference in a formula or as an argument in a function, simply include the worksheet reference and, if necessary, the workbook reference along with the cell or range reference. Remember that relative and absolute cell references behave the same in references to other worksheets and in external references as they do in standard references. You can also manually select a cell to include its reference in a formula or function. When inserting external references manually, the source workbook must also be open.

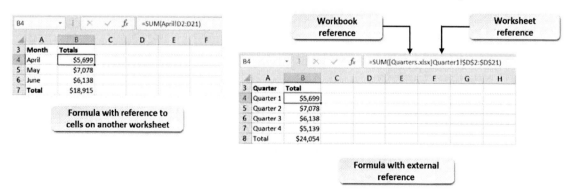

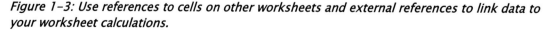

Figure 1–3: Use references to cells on other worksheets and external references to link data to your worksheet calculations.

Note: Whenever the source workbook for an external link or an external reference is closed, Excel automatically precedes it with the file path to the saved source Excel file. Excel does not display this file path when the source workbook is open. You don't ever have to manually type the file path into links, functions, or formulas.

Access the Checklist tile on your CHOICE Course screen for reference information and job aids on How to Use Linked Cells.

ACTIVITY 1-1
Creating Links

Data Files

C:\091057Data\Working with Multiple Worksheets and Workbooks\Develetech Sales.xlsx

C:\091057Data\Working with Multiple Worksheets and Workbooks\Q1 Sales.xlsx

C:\091057Data\Working with Multiple Worksheets and Workbooks\Q2 Sales.xlsx

C:\091057Data\Working with Multiple Worksheets and Workbooks\Q3 Sales.xlsx

C:\091057Data\Working with Multiple Worksheets and Workbooks\Q4 Sales.xlsx

Before You Begin

You are on the Windows desktop.

Scenario

You are a regional sales manager for Develetech Industries. Develetech is known as an innovative designer and producer of high-end televisions, video game consoles, laptop and tablet computers, and mobile phones.

You have a lot of data on several worksheets and different workbooks that you want to link to in order to streamline a report you are developing. You want to place total sales higher on the worksheet for more visibility, as well as highlight the sales of three salespersons with data from other worksheets. In addition, you are building a sales summary from four quarterly workbooks. You decide to create links to this data.

 Note: Activities may vary slightly if the software vendor has issued digital updates. Your instructor will notify you of any changes.

1. Open Excel and the **Develetech Sales.xlsx** workbook.
   a) Open Excel 2016.
   b) From the **Start** screen, select **Open Other Workbooks**.
   c) Select **Browse**.
   d) Navigate to **C:\091057Data\Working with Multiple Worksheets and Workbooks** and open the file **Develetech Sales.xlsx**.
   e) Save the file as *My Develetech Sales.xlsx* in the **Working with Multiple Worksheets and Workbooks** folder.

2. Create links to Total Sales and the sales totals of three salespersons.
   a) Verify that the **Data** worksheet is selected and that cell **B3** is selected.
   b) Type **=**
   c) Press **Ctrl+End** and if necessary, select cell **N2030** and press **Ctrl+Enter**.
   d) Verify that the total sales value is in cell **B3**.

B3	▾	⋮	✕	✓	*fx*	=N2030

◢	A	B
3	**Total Sales**	$7,692,385.53

e) Select cell **B5** and type *=*

f) Select the **Austin** worksheet and select cell **B3**.

g) Press **Ctrl+Enter**.

h) Verify that Austin's sales value is in cell **B5**.

B5		×	✓	*fx*	=Austin!B3

▲	A	B
5	Austin Sales	$966,867.78

i) Repeat creating the links for Scott and Watson sales in cells **B6** and **B7** respectively.

j) Verify the sales totals for each salesperson are displayed.

▲	A	B
1	Develetech Sales	
2		
3	Total Sales	$7,692,385.53
4		
5	Austin Sales	$966,867.78
6	Scott Sales	$823,271.33
7	Watson Sales	$791,766.32

3. Create external links to summarize the quarterly workbook data.

a) Select **File→Open** and in the **Working with Multiple Worksheets and Workbooks** folder, open the workbooks, **Q1 Sales.xlsx, Q2 Sales.xlsx, Q3 Sales.xlsx,** and **Q4 Sales.xlsx**.

b) Using the taskbar, switch back to **My Develetech Sales.xlsx**.

c) Select the **Summary** worksheet and verify that cell **B3** is selected and type *=*

d) Activate the **Q1 Sales.xlsx** workbook and select cell **D22** and press **Ctrl+Enter**.

e) Verify the Quarter 1 sales is displayed on the Summary worksheet.

B3		×	✓	*fx*	='[Q1 Sales.xlsx]Quarter1'!$D$22

▲	A	B	C	D	E
3	Quarter 1	$5,699			

f) Select cell **B4** and type *=*

g) Activate the **Q2 Sales.xlsx** workbook and select cell **D22** and press **Enter**.

 Note: You may have noticed that you are not using AutoFill to copy the formula and you cannot. This is because you are changing workbooks and each worksheet name corresponds to the quarter.

h) Verify that cell **B5** is selected and type *=*

i) Activate the **Q3 Sales.xlsx** workbook and select cell **D22** and press **Enter**.

j) Verify that cell **B6** is selected and type *=*

k) Activate the **Q4 Sales.xlsx** workbook and select cell **D22** and press **Enter**.

l) Verify the quarterly sales values appear.

	A	B
1	**Quarterly Sales Summary**	
2		
3	Quarter 1	$5,699
4	Quarter 2	$6,180
5	Quarter 3	$6,113
6	Quarter 4	$5,520
7	**Yearly Total**	**$23,512**

4. Save and close the **My Develetech Sales.xlsx** workbook, but keep the quarterly sales files open.

TOPIC B

Use 3-D References

It's not uncommon for various groups of people or various departments throughout an organization to keep similar data in workbooks based on templates. For example, everyone may use the same template to track budgets or time-off requests, regardless of department. Or, you may simply track quarterly sales by using the same basic worksheet layout each quarter. Although it's useful to have your data organized by specific general categories like this, you will also likely need to see the big picture of what all of the various worksheets contain. And, you will still likely need to analyze this data to some degree, so simply adding up the totals for each worksheet in one location may not be much help.

Fortunately, Excel 2016 provides you with the ability to summarize the data from a series of worksheets by applying calculations across all of them. In the previous topic, you learned how to create internal and external links. This topic builds on that ability by building summary calculations from multiple worksheets or multiple workbooks in a single location.

Grouped Worksheets

Grouping worksheets can be very helpful when setting up files for 3-D references. Excel 2016 allows you to temporarily group worksheets together so you can add, revise, and format them simultaneously. For example, if you group a series of worksheets and then add the value **100** to cell **A1** in the visible worksheet, you enter that value in cell **A1** on all worksheets in the group. This can be a handy way, for example, of setting up a number of worksheets with the same labels, sections, and so on.

Essentially, this is the same as selecting multiple cells on a worksheet to apply the same formatting to each cell. You can group contiguous worksheet tabs by selecting the first tab, pressing and holding the **Shift** key, and then selecting the last tab. You can group non-contiguous worksheet tabs by pressing and holding down the **Ctrl** key and selecting the desired tabs. Although you can rename worksheet tabs one at a time only, you can move, hide, or apply color to a group of worksheets simultaneously. When worksheets are grouped, the word "Group" appears appended to the file name of the workbook on the title bar. To ungroup worksheets, select a worksheet not part of the group or right-click one of the grouped worksheets and select **Ungroup Sheets**.

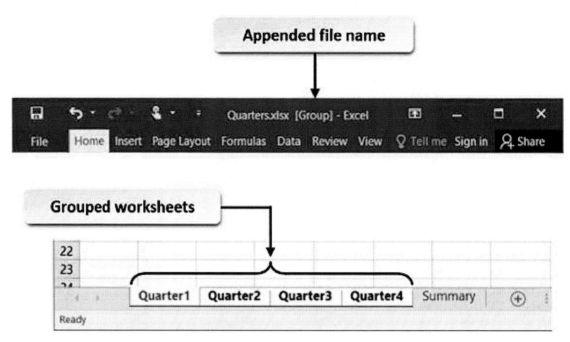

Figure 1-4: The four quarter worksheets grouped.

3-D References

Imagine a stack of printed worksheets, one atop the next, with all of the data on each sheet lining up with the others. The column and row labels are the same, the datasets are the same size and are in the same location, and the data entered into each cell corresponds to that of the other cells stacked above or below it on the various worksheets. Now, imagine you place a worksheet on the top of the stack with the same column and row labels, but no data in the other cells. Suppose you wanted to populate each of the empty cells in the top worksheet with a summary of the cell data from the other aligning cells. Well, in Excel 2016, you can do just that by using a powerful feature called *3-D references*. A 3-D reference is simply a reference to the same cell across a range of worksheets. For example, if you have a workbook containing three worksheets and you want to reference cell **B3** on all three of them simultaneously, you would use a 3-D reference to tell Excel to execute some function on all three instances of cell **B3**.

 Note: 3-D references work only on worksheets contained in the same workbook. They are typically useful only if the datasets on all worksheets are entered in the exact same location and in the exact same layout.

3-D references combine the use of a worksheet reference and the range reference operator, which you'll recall is the colon (:). So, in the example mentioned previously, if your workbook contains worksheets **Sheet1**, **Sheet2**, and **Sheet3**, and you want to reference cell **B3** in all three worksheets, your 3-D reference would be: **Sheet1:Sheet3!B3**.

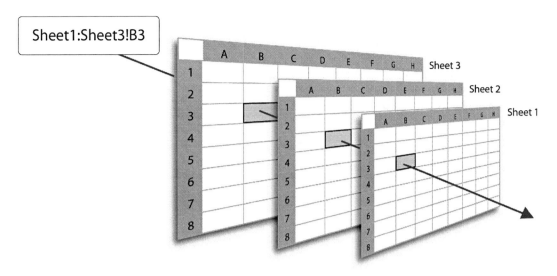

Figure 1-5: 3-D references refer to the corresponding cell values in a range of stacked worksheets.

3-D References in Summary Functions

You can combine 3-D references with any of the summary functions you would normally use to reference a flat, or 2-D, cell or range. So, if your goal is to add all of the values in cell **B3** on all three worksheets from **Sheet1** to **Sheet3**, you would enter the following function:

=SUM(Sheet1:Sheet3!B3)

Or, suppose you wanted to determine the average of the values in those cells. Your function would look like this:

=AVERAGE(Sheet1:Sheet3!B3)

> **Note:** When you type a 3-D reference, you may have to enclose the worksheet reference in single quotation marks (' '), which should not include the exclamation point (!). This may be necessary as worksheet names can contain spaces or a blend of numbers and letters. Example: **=SUM('Sales Data1:Sales Data2'!D4)**.

In both of these examples, the range reference **Sheet1:Sheet3!** is telling Excel to look at the values in the corresponding cell in each of the worksheets from **Sheet1** through **Sheet3**. But, there is something really important for you to keep in mind here. The 3-D range reference has nothing to do with the sheet names. In this example, Excel will look for values in **Sheet1**, **Sheet3**, and every other worksheet physically between them in the workbook. So, if you have a worksheet in between them named **Summary**, Excel will look for the corresponding value in that worksheet. But if **Sheet2** is somewhere to the right or to the left of the worksheet range referenced, Excel will ignore those values. Take a look at the following example.

‹ ›	Sheet1	**Summary**	**Sheet3**	Sheet2	Sheet4	⊕
Ready						

Figure 1-6: Spreadsheet example of sheet physical location versus label.

Here, the 3-D reference **Sheet1:Sheet3** would include the corresponding cell value from the **Summary** worksheet, but not from the **Sheet2** worksheet.

Note: You can manually select a worksheet range when entering a 3-D reference in much the same way you manually select a cell or a range reference. To do this, you select the first worksheet in the desired range, press and hold the **Shift** key, and then select the last worksheet in the desired range. Once you have selected the desired worksheet range, you can manually select a cell or a range reference as you normally would.

You can also combine range references for cells and range references for worksheets to summarize a range of data on multiple worksheets simultaneously. However, remember that this will not return the summarized values for each set of corresponding cells individually. Take a look at this function as an example:

=AVERAGE(Sheet1:Sheet3!A1:D4)

Although this function will return the average of all values in the range **A1:D4** for all three worksheets, it will return that value in a single cell. You can, however, use the AutoFill feature to drag a single formula containing a 3-D reference and a relative cell reference across a range to summarize each set of corresponding cells individually. For example, if you want to find the total for each set of corresponding cells in the range **A1:E10** across the same three worksheets, you would enter the following function in a single cell:

=SUM(Sheet1:Sheet3!A1)

Notice the use of a relative cell reference. Now you would select the cell you entered the function into and use the **fill handle** to drag the formula across a range that is the same size as the original ranges. Although you may want to do this in the range **A1:E10** on a new worksheet to make it easier to view and understand your data, you can do this in any range that is the correct size.

Access the Checklist tile on your CHOICE Course screen for reference information and job aids on How to Use 3-D References.

ACTIVITY 1-2
Using 3-D References

Data File

C:\091057Data\Working with Multiple Worksheets and Workbooks\Summary.xlsx

Before You Begin

The files Q1 Sales.xlsx, Q2 Sales.xlsx, Q3 Sales.xlsx, and Q4 Sales.xlsx are open.

Scenario

Continuing your work on summarizing sales data, your manager has given you a workbook containing quarterly sales totals. As you explore the workbook, you find the totals are in the same location on each of the quarter worksheets. You decide to use a 3-D formula to calculate the quarterly sales total and the average quarterly sales.

1. Open the **Summary.xlsx** workbook.
   a) In Excel, open the workbook **Summary.xlsx**.
   b) Save the file as *My Summary.xlsx* in the **Working with Multiple Worksheets and Workbooks** folder.

2. Create a 3-D formula totalling the quarterly sales.
   a) Examine the quarter worksheets and note that they are constructed identically.
   b) Select the **Summary** worksheet, and cell **B3** if necessary.
   c) Type *=SUM(*
   d) Select the **Quarter1** worksheet and then hold **Shift** and select the **Quarter4** worksheet.
   e) Select cell **D22** and press **Ctrl+Enter**.
   f) Verify the quarterly sales total was added to cell B3.

B3	▾	⋮	×	✓	f_x	=SUM(Quarter1:Quarter4!D22)		
◢	A		B	C	D	E	F	
1	Yearly Total							
2								
3	Quarterly Sales Total		$24,054					

3. Create a 3-D formula averaging quarterly sales.
   a) Select cell **B4** and type *=AVERAGE(*
   b) Select the **Quarter1** worksheet and then hold **Shift** and select the **Quarter4** worksheet.
   c) Select cell **D22** and press **Ctrl+Enter**.

d) Verify the average quarterly sales value is calculated in cell **B4**.

B4		× ✓ *fx*	=AVERAGE(Quarter1:Quarter4!D22)			
	A	**B**	**C**	**D**	**E**	**F**
1	**Yearly Total**					
2						
3	**Quarterly Sales Total**	$24,054				
4	**Average Quarterly Sales**	$6,014				

4. Save and close the **My Summary.xlsx** workbook and keep the quarterly sales files open.

TOPIC C

Consolidate Data

The ability to use 3-D references to summarize datasets with identical layouts is a powerful, handy feature. But, what if you need to summarize data from datasets that aren't laid out in precisely the same way? Or, what if you want to summarize data from a number of worksheets in different workbooks? Life isn't always neat and tidy, and, unfortunately, the same can be said of workbook data.

The good news is that Excel 2016 enables you to summarize data from multiple worksheets regardless of whether or not the data is in the same location on each worksheet, or even if the worksheets are in the same workbook. This means you can get a birds-eye view of your overall data picture without having to painstakingly copy and paste your raw data into the same workbook and modify the layout so that it all matches.

Data Consolidation

Data consolidation is another means of summarizing data from other worksheets and workbooks, as you learned by creating links and 3-D formulas in the previous topics. Excel 2016 enables you to consolidate data based on either relative cell positions in the various source datasets or by categories, which are based on row and column labels. You can summarize consolidated data by using summary and statistical functions available in Excel.

	Product	Quantity	Price	Total Sales
1 Consolidated Sales				
8	4489	58	$23.00	$1,334.00
13	4865	48	$40.00	$1,920.00
18	2030	17	$39.00	$663.00
23	4503	48	$20.00	$960.00
28	4476	27	$24.00	$648.00
33	4457	59	$45.00	$2,655.00
38	4779	24	$33.00	$792.00
43	3640	49	$39.00	$1,911.00
48	1665	57	$31.00	$1,767.00
53	4269	38	$29.00	$1,102.00
58	1847	22	$24.00	$528.00
63	1389	38	$20.00	$760.00
68	4547	57	$26.00	$1,482.00
73	4899	25	$47.00	$1,175.00
78	4197	37	$34.00	$1,258.00
83	4495	29	$10.00	$290.00
88	3840	29	$41.00	$1,189.00
93	2766	40	$31.00	$1,240.00
98	3551	38	$26.00	$988.00
103	3366	34	$25.00	$850.00

Figure 1–7: Excel creates consolidated datasets that are linked to the source data as outlines.

Although source datasets don't have to be in precisely the same location on all worksheets, or even contain the same number of columns or rows, it's a best practice to ensure your data is structured in approximately the same manner. For example, if you consolidate data by category using column labels as the category indicators, the columns don't have to appear in the same location within the various sources and the columns don't even have to appear in the same order, but the various datasets should include the same column labels. And all data ranges that you enter into a consolidated dataset by category must be contiguous, meaning there can be no empty rows or columns. If your original data is non-contiguous, you can consolidate it by using relative cell positions as long as you enter each non-contiguous range separately.

You have the option of linking your consolidated dataset to the original data sources. This way, your consolidated dataset will update whenever the original source data is updated. Keep in mind, however, that if you link your consolidated data to the sources, Excel automatically creates the consolidated dataset as an outline with the detail entries collapsed.

The Consolidate Dialog Box

You use the **Consolidate** dialog box to determine which source datasets Excel will summarize in the consolidated dataset, which summary function it will use to summarize the data, and how it will organize the consolidated dataset. You can access the **Consolidate** dialog box by selecting **Data→Data Tools→Consolidate**.

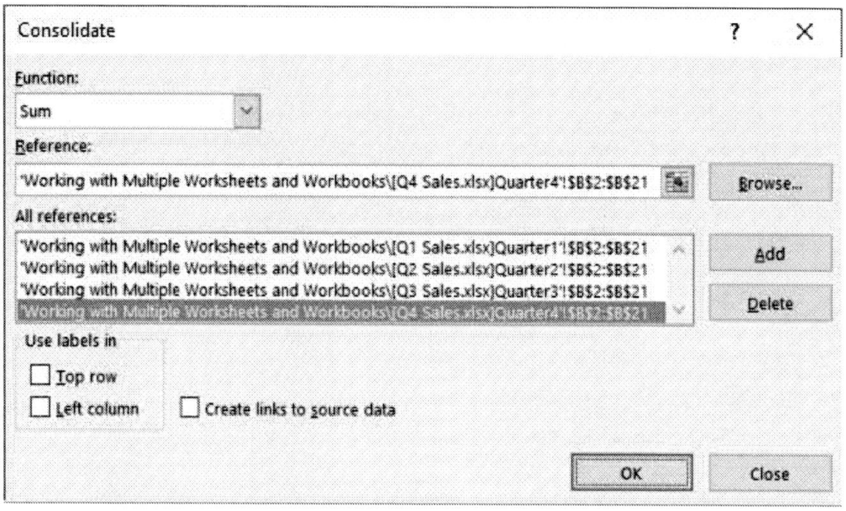

Figure 1-8: The Consolidate dialog box.

The following table describes the various elements of the **Consolidate** dialog box.

Consolidate Dialog Box Element	Description
Function drop-down menu	Use this to select the function Excel will use to consolidate the source data.
Reference field	Use this to enter each range of data you wish to add to the consolidated dataset.
All references list	Displays a list of all of the ranges included in the consolidated dataset.
Browse button	Opens the **Browse** dialog box, enabling you to search for workbook files that aren't currently open to include in the consolidated dataset.
Add button	Adds the range currently displayed in the **Reference** field to the **All references** list.
Delete button	Removes the currently selected range reference from the **All references** list.

Consolidate Dialog Box Element	Description
Top row check box	Check this if you include column labels in your source data ranges and you want Excel to organize your consolidated dataset by category according to the column labels.
Left column check box	Check this if you include row labels in your source data ranges and you want Excel to organize your consolidated dataset by category according to the row labels.
Create links to source data check box	Check this if you want Excel to create links to the source data in the consolidated dataset. Linking the consolidated dataset automatically structures it as an outline.

Note: If you want Excel to use both column and row labels to organize the consolidated dataset by category, check both the **Top row** and the **Left column** check boxes. You must include both column and row labels in the source data ranges to do this. If you want Excel to organize the consolidated dataset according to relative cell positions within the source datasets, leave both of these check boxes unchecked.

Access the Checklist tile on your CHOICE Course screen for reference information and job aids on How to Consolidate Data.

ACTIVITY 1–3
Consolidating Data

Data File
C:\091057Data\Working with Multiple Worksheets and Workbooks\Consolidate.xlsx

Before You Begin
The quarterly sales files, Q1 Sales.xlsx, Q2 Sales.xlsx, Q3 Sales.xlsx, and Q4 Sales.xlsx are open.

Scenario
You were able to total the quarterly sales and you now want to summarize the quantities sold from each of the quarters. You decide to consolidate the quarterly quantities sold to the Consolidation workbook.

1. Open the **Consolidate.xlsx** workbook.
   a) In Excel, open the file **Consolidate.xlsx**.
   b) Save the file as *My Consolidate.xlsx* in the **Working with Multiple Worksheets and Workbooks** folder.

2. Examine the quarterly sales files noting that the Product column contains the same products but not in the same order.
   a) Using the taskbar, switch to **Q1 Sales.xlsx** and note the order of the Product column.
   b) Using the taskbar, switch to **Q2 Sales.xlsx** and note the order of the Product column.
   c) Repeat the process for the **Q3 Sales.xlsx** and **Q4 Sales.xlsx** files.
   d) Switch back to the **My Consolidate.xlsx** file.

3. Consolidate the quantity of products sold from each of the quarterly sales files.
   a) Select the range **B3:C23**.
   b) Select **Data→Data Tools→Consolidate**.
   c) In the **Consolidate** dialog box, verify that **Sum** is the Function selected.
   d) Verify the cursor is in the **Reference** field.
   e) Select **View→Window→Switch Windows** and select the **Q1 Sales.xlsx** workbook.
   f) On the Quarter1 worksheet, select the range **A1:B21**.

g) In the **Consolidate** dialog box, verify the reference to '[Q1 Sales.xlsx]Quarter1'!$A$1:$B$21 and select **Add**.

4. Add the references for the remaining quarters.

   a) Select **View→Window→Switch Windows** and select the **Q2 Sales.xlsx** workbook.
   b) Select the range **A1:B21** and in the **Consolidate** dialog box, select **Add** to add the reference to the **All references** list box.
   c) Repeat adding references to Q3 Sales.xlsx and Q4 Sales.xlsx for the same range.
   d) Verify the four quarter references are listed in the **All references** list box.

5. Create links to source data and complete the consolidation.

   a) In the **Consolidate** dialog box, select the **Top row**, **Left column**, and **Create links to source data** check boxes and select **OK**.

b) Switch to the **My Consolidate.xlsx** workbook, if necessary, and observe the quantities for each product from all the workbooks have been consolidated.

	A	B	C	D	E	F	G
1	Consolidated Sales						
2							
3		Product		Quantity	Price	Total Sales	
8		4489		58	$23.00	$1,334.00	
13		4865		48	$40.00	$1,920.00	
18		2030		17	$39.00	$663.00	
23		4503		48	$20.00	$960.00	
28		4476		27	$24.00	$648.00	
33		4457		59	$45.00	$2,655.00	
38		4779		24	$33.00	$792.00	
43		3640		49	$39.00	$1,911.00	
48		1665		57	$31.00	$1,767.00	
53		4269		38	$29.00	$1,102.00	
58		1847		22	$24.00	$528.00	
63		1389		38	$20.00	$760.00	
68		4547		57	$26.00	$1,482.00	
73		4899		25	$47.00	$1,175.00	
78		4197		37	$34.00	$1,258.00	
83		4495		29	$10.00	$290.00	
88		3840		29	$41.00	$1,189.00	
93		2766		40	$31.00	$1,240.00	
98		3551		38	$26.00	$988.00	
103		3366		34	$25.00	$850.00	
104							

6. View the details of the consolidated data.

   a) In the **Outline** pane, to the left of the column headings, select **2** to expand the outline and show details.

   b) Select cell **D4** and observe the **Formula Bar** reference to **Q1 Sales.xlsx**.

D4			fx	='[Q1 Sales.xlsx]Quarter1'!$B$8

	A	B	C	D	E	F	G	H
3		Product		Quantity	Price	Total Sales		
4			Q1 Sales	20				
5			Q2 Sales	19				
6			Q3 Sales	14				
7			Q4 Sales	5				
8		4489		58	$23.00	$1,334.00		

   c) Examine the source for cells **D5**, **D6**, and **D7**.

7. Save the workbook **My Consolidation.xlsx** and close all open workbooks. Keep Excel open.

Summary

In this lesson, you worked with a number of worksheets and workbooks simultaneously in order to analyze data from a variety of sources in a single location. By taking advantage of Excel's ability to reference data from a variety of sources, you'll capture the full potential of the wide range of data available in your organization. And, you'll do so without the extra time and effort it would take to manually copy or move the source data, a task that could be nearly impossible in large organizations. In addition to saving time and effort, you'll also ensure that errors are kept to a minimum, maintaining the integrity of both your raw data and your analysis.

Which method of simultaneously working with multiple worksheets and workbooks do you think will help you the most with your daily tasks? Why?

Can you think of a time when having your workbook cells linked to the source data would have saved you time, effort, and hassle?

 Note: Check your CHOICE Course screen for opportunities to interact with your classmates, peers, and the larger CHOICE online community about the topics covered in this course or other topics you are interested in. From the Course screen you can also access available resources for a more continuous learning experience.

2 Using Lookup Functions and Formula Auditing

Lesson Time: 1 hour, 15 minutes

Lesson Introduction

The formulas and functions within Microsoft® Office Excel® 2016 provide you with a robust set of options for performing complex calculations on the data in your workbooks. But on their own, they may not always perform the precise calculations you need them to. For example, you may need a function to reference a value from another dataset based on some particular criteria. But, how do you tell the function how to look that up? Or perhaps you need one of your arguments to be the result of another formula or function. As your workbooks become larger and more complex, errors can crop up and searching for the cause of errors or unexpected results and troubleshooting your formulas and functions can become a nightmare.

Fortunately, Excel provides you with a number of options for dealing with these, and many other situations. But doing so requires an understanding of a new set of Excel functions, Lookup functions, and a deeper understanding of function syntax. By investing the time it takes to elevate your understanding of how these functions work and how they work together, you'll begin to develop the ability to create incredibly complex functions and formulas that can perform any number of calculations. In addition, you will be able to audit your workbook content to find, troubleshoot, and correct a number of different errors. Developing the skills you need to perform these audits can save you tremendous amounts of time, effort, and frustration when errors arise and will give you the peace of mind that comes with knowing you can trust your data and analysis.

Lesson Objectives

In this lesson, you will use Lookup functions and audit formulas. You will:

- Use Lookup functions.

- Trace cells.

- Watch and evaluate formulas.

TOPIC A

Use Lookup Functions

So, you've collected a massive amount of data about your operations, upon which you can perform an amazing variety of analysis. But, what if you want quick access to just a particular bit of data? In some cases, you may be able to sort, filter, or even search for it. But suppose you don't know what the value is. For example, what if you need to find out who employee 1287's manager is or in which region he or she works? If you don't know the answer you're looking for, you don't know what search criteria to enter. Or perhaps you need to enter the total number of units sold for a particular product into a formula. Although you could search for the product and look up the value yourself, you wouldn't want to do this for multiple products over and over.

Fortunately, Excel 2016 enables you to look up such values, even in massive datasets, with relative ease. By using a set of functions known as Lookup functions, you'll be able to look up or include in a formula or function any one particular entry in any dataset. This level of functionality can quickly give you a detailed view of how any one individual value contributes to the overall operation of your organization. This can help you make clear, informed decisions that affect large-scale operations based on just a single chunk of data.

Lookup Functions

In Excel, Lookup functions do exactly what you'd think they would; they look up some value. Specifically, Lookup functions search through a particular dataset to return a particular value based on some criteria. Take a look at this simple example of how you might use a Lookup function.

	A	B	C	D	E
1	Employee ID	Department	Region	Manager	Salary
2	1003	Engineering	Midwest	Dandridge, Ray	$73,450.00
3					
4	Employee ID	Department	Region	Manager	Salary
5	1001	Marketing	Southeast	French, Ernestine	Commission
6	1002	Information Technology	Northeast	Redd, Randal	$72,300.00
7	1003	Engineering	Midwest	Dandridge, Ray	$73,450.00
8	1004	Information Technology	West	Redd, Randal	$55,000.00
9	1005	Marketing	Southwest	French, Ernestine	Commission
10	1006	Engineering	Southwest	Dandridge, Ray	$60,500.00
11	1007	Marketing	Southeast	French, Ernestine	Commission
12	1008	Engineering	Southeast	Dandridge, Ray	$83,660.00
13	1009	Accounting	Northeast	Gosselin, Theo	$87,000.00
14	1010	Marketing	Northeast	French, Ernestine	Commission

Figure 2-1: An example of a Lookup function.

In this example, the Lookup function is looking up employee 1003's salary. A Lookup function can identify the range **A4:E14**, search down column **A** until it finds **1003**, and then look across the row to the **Salary** column to return the result $73,450.00. Lookup functions can perform other tasks as well. For example, they can look across a row to find the lookup value, and then count down rows to return another value. They can return a value in the equivalent location as another value in separate ranges. Or, they can return a value's place in a range. The particular Lookup function in the given example, which is in cell **E2**, references cell **A2**. So, for any employee ID a user enters, the function will return the salary.

As is the case with all Excel functions, the key to leveraging Lookup functions is understanding function syntax. Let's take a look at the syntax for some of the most commonly used Lookup functions.

The VLOOKUP Function

Syntax: =VLOOKUP(**lookup_value**, **table_array**, **col_index_num**, [range_lookup])

You can use the VLOOKUP function to search down the first column of a dataset to find a specified value and then return the value from a cell in any column in the row that contains the specified value. The following is a description of the function's arguments.

VLOOKUP Function Argument	Description
lookup_value	This is the value the function will search for in the first column of the specified dataset. The **lookup_value** argument can either be a hard-coded value or a reference to the value in another cell.
table_array	This argument specifies the dataset the VLOOKUP function searches. This argument can be a range reference, a defined name, or an array constant.
col_index_num	This argument is a positive whole number that specifies the column number from the dataset that the function will return a value from. If you enter 3, the function returns the value from the cell in the third column of the same row as the lookup value. If you enter a 4, it returns the value from the cell in the fourth column of the same row. Note that if you enter 1 for this argument, the function will return the lookup value itself as that is the value in the first column of the specified dataset.
[range_lookup]	This is an optional argument that determines whether the function looks for an exact match of the lookup value or an approximate equivalent. If you enter the value FALSE for this argument, the function will look for only exact matches. If you omit this argument or enter a value of TRUE, the function will look for either an exact match or an approximate match. An approximate match is the largest value that is less than the value of the lookup value. If the **[range-lookup]** argument is FALSE, the values in the first column (the one containing the lookup value) do not need to be sorted. In all other cases, they must be sorted in ascending order.

Note: When the lookup value in the first column is a text label, it's a best practice to enter the **[range_lookup]** argument as FALSE. This will only return a value based on an exact match. And, if you hard code the **lookup_value** argument, as opposed to using a cell reference, you must enclose the text string in double quotation marks (" ").

Note: Like with most logical values, you can simply enter 1 for TRUE or 0 for FALSE in the **[range_lookup]** argument.

	A	B	C	D	E
1	Employee ID	Department	Region	Manager	Salary
2	1010	Marketing	Northeast	French, Ernestine	Commission
3					
4	Employee ID	Department	Region	Manager	Salary
5	1001	Marketing	Southeast	French, Ernestine	Commission
6	1002	Information Technology	Northeast	Redd, Randal	$72,300.00
7	1003	Engineering	Midwest	Dandridge, Ray	$73,450.00
8	1004	Information Technology	West	Redd, Randal	$55,000.00
9	1005	Marketing	Southwest	French, Ernestine	Commission
10	1006	Engineering	Southwest	Dandridge, Ray	$60,500.00
11	1007	Marketing	Southeast	French, Ernestine	Commission
12	1008	Engineering	Southeast	Dandridge, Ray	$83,660.00
13	1009	Accounting	Northeast	Gosselin, Theo	$87,000.00
14	1010	Marketing	Northeast	French, Ernestine	Commission

Figure 2-2: The following examples refer to this simple dataset.

To Return This Value	Enter This Function
Commission	=VLOOKUP(1005, A4:E14,5)
Northeast	=VLOOKUP(1002, A4:E14,3)
French, Ernestine	=VLOOKUP(A2, Data,4)
	This example assumes the dataset has been assigned the defined name Data.

The LOOKUP Function

While most Excel users use the VLOOKUP function, the LOOKUP function may be useful as well. There are two forms of the LOOKUP function, the vector form and the array form. The vector form searches for a specified value within one *vector*, that is a single row or column and then returns the equivalent value in a second vector. The array form of the LOOKUP function searches in either the first row or the first column of an array (a range that contains both columns and rows), and then returns the corresponding value from the last row or column of the same array. It is also recommended that you use VLOOKUP or HLOOKUP instead of the array form.

Syntax Vector Form: =LOOKUP(**lookup_value**, **lookup_vector**, [result_vector])

Syntax Array Form: =LOOKUP(**lookup_value**, **array**)

The LOOKUP function can serve one of two purposes depending on the syntax form you use. The following table describes the LOOKUP function's arguments.

LOOKUP Function Argument	Description
lookup_value	Specifies the value the function searches for. This argument can be a numeric value, a text string, a logical value, a defined name, or a cell reference.
lookup_vector or array	When using the vector form of the LOOKUP function, this argument defines the first vector (the one the function will search through to find the value specified in the **lookup_value** argument). In the function's array form, this argument specifies the entire range the function will search (when using the array form, the function returns the result from the same range in which it searches for the lookup value).

LOOKUP Function Argument	Description
[result_vector]	Include this argument only when using the vector form of the LOOKUP function. This specifies the vector from which Excel will return the result. The result vector must be the same size as the lookup vector.

 Note: When using the vector form of the LOOKUP function, the values in the lookup vector should be sorted in either ascending or alphabetical order. Otherwise, the function may not work properly. The same is true of the values in the first row or column (depending on which is being searched) of an array when using the array form of the function.

The HLOOKUP Function

Syntax: =HLOOKUP(**lookup_value**, **table_array**, **row_index_num**, [range_lookup])

 Note: You will likely find yourself using the VLOOKUP function far more often than the HLOOKUP function, as most datasets are configured with individual records in rows.

You can use the HLOOKUP function to search across the first row of a dataset to find a specified value, and then return the value from a cell in any row of the column that contains the specified value. Here is a description of the function's arguments.

HLOOKUP Function Argument	Description
lookup_value	This is the value the function will search for in the first row of the specified dataset. The **lookup_value** argument can either be a hard-coded value or a reference to the value in another cell.
table_array	This argument specifies the dataset the HLOOKUP function searches. This argument can be a range reference, a defined name, or an array constant.
row_index_num	This argument is a positive whole number that specifies the row number from the dataset that the function will return a value from. If you enter 3, the function returns the value from the cell in the third row of the same column as the lookup value. If you enter a 4, it returns the value from the cell in the fourth row of the same column. Note that if you enter 1 for this argument, the function will return the lookup value itself, as that is the value in the first row of the specified dataset.
[range_lookup]	This is an optional argument that determines whether the function looks for an exact match of the lookup value or an approximate equivalent. If you enter the value FALSE for this argument, the function will look for only exact matches. If you omit this argument or enter a value of TRUE, the function will look for either an exact match or an approximate match. An approximate match is the largest value that is less than the value of the lookup value. If the **[range-lookup]** argument is FALSE, the values in the first row (the one containing the lookup value) do not need to be sorted. In all other cases, they must be sorted in ascending order.

Note: When the lookup value in the first row is a text label, it's a best practice to enter the **[range_lookup]** argument as FALSE. This will only return a value based on an exact match. And if you hard code the **lookup_value** argument, as opposed to using a cell reference, you must enclose the text string in double quotation marks (" ").

Note: As with most logical values, you can simply enter 1 for TRUE or 0 for FALSE in the **[range_lookup]** argument.

	A	B	C	D	E	F
1	Employee ID	Department	Region	Manager	Salary	
2	1003	Engineering	Midwest	Dandridge, Ray	$73,450.00	
3						
4	Employee ID	1001	1002	1003	1004	1005
5	Department	Marketing	Information Technology	Engineering	Information Technology	Marketing
6	Region	Southeast	Northeast	Midwest	West	Southwest
7	Manager	French, Ernestine	Redd, Randal	Dandridge, Ray	Redd, Randal	French, Ernestine
8	Salary	Commission	$72,300.00	$73,450.00	$55,000.00	Commission

Figure 2–3: The following examples refer to this simple dataset.

To Return This Value	Enter This Function
$73,450.00	=HLOOKUP(1003,A4:F8,5,FALSE)
Dandridge, Ray	=HLOOKUP(A2,A4:F8,4,0)
Engineering	=HLOOKUP(A2, A4:F8, 2)

The MATCH Function

Syntax: =MATCH(**lookup_value**, **lookup_array**, [match_type])

This function returns the numerical representation of a value's place within a single-row or a single-column range (a vector). For example, consider this list: blue, red, green, orange, yellow. If you enter this list in a range of cells and then ask the MATCH function to look up "orange," it will return the value 4 because "orange" is the fourth item in the list. This function is often used to return, for example, an item's row number for use as an argument in other Lookup functions. The following is a description of the function's arguments.

MATCH Function Argument	Description
lookup_value	This is the value the function will search for in the specified range. The **lookup_value** argument can be either a hard-coded value or a reference to a cell containing a value. If you are entering a text string for this argument, you must enclose the value in double quotation marks (" ").
lookup_array	This argument specifies the range the function will search. This must represent a single row or a single column (a vector) of values that may have to be sorted in either ascending or descending order to avoid errors.

MATCH Function Argument	Description
[match_type]	This argument determines whether the MATCH function looks for an exact match to the lookup value or an approximate match. This function has three possible values: –1, 0, and 1. • The value 1 tells the function to look for the largest value that is less than or equal to the lookup value. If you enter 1 for the **[match_type]** argument, the values in the **lookup_array** argument must be sorted in ascending order. 1 is the default value for this argument, so it's the same as omitting the argument entirely. • The value 0 tells the function to look only for an exact match of the lookup value. In this case, the values do not need to be sorted in any particular order. • The value –1 tells the function to look for the smallest value that is greater than or equal to the lookup value. If you enter this value for the **[match_type]** argument, the values in the **lookup-array** argument must be sorted in descending order.

	A	B	C	D	E
1	**Employee ID**	**Department**	**Region**	**Manager**	**Salary**
2	1007	Information Technology	Southeast	French, Ernestine	$60,750.00
3					
4	**Match**				
5	11	3	2	2	7
6					
7	**Employee ID**	**Department**	**Region**	**Manager**	**Salary**
8	1001	Marketing	Southeast	French, Ernestine	Commission
9	1002	Information Technology	Northeast	Redd, Randal	$72,300.00
10	1003	Engineering	Midwest	Dandridge, Ray	$73,450.00
11	1004	Information Technology	West	Redd, Randal	$55,000.00
12	1005	Marketing	Southwest	French, Ernestine	Commission
13	1006	Engineering	Southwest	Dandridge, Ray	$60,500.00
14	1007	Marketing	Southeast	French, Ernestine	Commission
15	1008	Engineering	Southeast	Dandridge, Ray	$83,660.00
16	1009	Accounting	Northeast	Gosselin, Theo	$87,000.00
17	1010	Marketing	Northeast	French, Ernestine	Commission

Figure 2-4: The following examples refer to this simple dataset.

To Return This Value	Enter This Function
11	=MATCH(1010,A7:A17,0)
3	=MATCH("Information Technology",B7:B17,0)
7	=MATCH(E2,E7:E17,1)

The INDEX Function

Syntax: =INDEX(**array**, **row_number**, [column_name])

> **Note:** The syntax presented here is for the array form of the INDEX function. There is also a less commonly used version of the INDEX function called the reference form. The reference form of this function returns a cell reference as opposed to a particular value. You can review the reference form's syntax in Excel Help or at **Office.com**.

The INDEX function returns the value in a particular row and/or column of a given range of cells. If the specified range of cells contains both multiple rows and columns, you must specify both a row and a column for the function to search. In these cases, the INDEX function returns the value in the cell at the intersection of the specified row and column. If the specified range of cells represents a single row, you need only specify a column reference (all of the cells are in the same row). The opposite is true of a range that represents only a single column. Here is a description of the function's arguments.

INDEX Function Argument	Description
array	This argument specifies the dataset that the function will search.
row_number	This argument is a positive whole number that specifies the row number from the specified dataset the function will look in.
[column_name]	This argument is a positive whole number that specifies the column number from the specified dataset the function will look in.

Note: Although the INDEX function's syntax indicates the **row_number** argument is required and the **[column_name]** argument is optional, this isn't necessarily true. When the dataset specified in the **array** argument contains multiple rows and multiple columns, both arguments are required. If the dataset is a single row, only the **[column_name]** argument is required. If the dataset is a single column, only the **row_number** argument is required.

	A	B	C	D	E
1	**Employee ID**	**Department**	**Region**	**Manager**	**Salary**
2	1010	Marketing	Southeast	Redd, Randal	$83,660.00
3					
4	**Employee ID**	**Department**	**Region**	**Manager**	**Salary**
5	1001	Marketing	Southeast	French, Ernestine	Commission
6	1002	Information Technology	Northeast	Redd, Randal	$72,300.00
7	1003	Engineering	Midwest	Dandridge, Ray	$73,450.00
8	1004	Information Technology	West	Redd, Randal	$55,000.00
9	1005	Marketing	Southwest	French, Ernestine	Commission
10	1006	Engineering	Southwest	Dandridge, Ray	$60,500.00
11	1007	Marketing	Southeast	French, Ernestine	Commission
12	1008	Engineering	Southeast	Dandridge, Ray	$83,660.00
13	1009	Accounting	Northeast	Gosselin, Theo	$87,000.00
14	1010	Marketing	Northeast	French, Ernestine	Commission

Figure 2-5: The following examples refer to this simple dataset.

To Return This Value	Enter This Function
Redd, Randal	=INDEX(A4:E14,5,4)
1010	=INDEX(A4:A14,11)
83660	=INDEX(E4:E14,9)

The TRANSPOSE Function

Syntax: =TRANSPOSE(**array**)

You use the TRANSPOSE function to switch the orientation of a dataset. When you use the TRANSPOSE function to rearrange a dataset, Excel creates the first column in the transposed dataset out of the first row of the original dataset, the second column out of the second row, and so forth until the entire dataset is transposed.

Using the TRANSPOSE function is similar to using the **Transpose** paste option, but there are several important differences. The main advantage to using the TRANSPOSE function is that it maintains an active, dynamic link to the original dataset, which the **Transpose** paste option does not do. So, any values you update in the original dataset, reflect in the transposed dataset. The other key point to understand is that the TRANSPOSE function only works as an array function. So, you must enter it into the entire destination range simultaneously, and you must press **Ctrl+Shift+Enter** to enter the function. Keep in mind the destination range must contain the same number of rows as the original dataset has columns, and it must have the same number of columns as the original dataset has rows.

The only argument for the TRANSPOSE function is the **array** argument, which identifies the range of the original dataset.

F1	▼	:	×	✓	*fx*	{=TRANSPOSE(A1:D6)}				
	A	B	C	D	E	F	G	H	I	J	K
1	Employee	Salary	Rate	Commission		Employee	1001	1002	1003	1004	1005
2	1001	$92,119.00	5.00%	$4,605.95		Salary	$92,119.00	$76,615.00	$98,157.00	$85,616.00	$73,131.00
3	1002	$76,615.00	8.00%	$6,129.20		Rate	5.00%	8.00%	7.00%	5.00%	6.00%
4	1003	$98,157.00	7.00%	$6,870.99		Commission	$4,605.95	$6,129.20	$6,870.99	$4,280.80	$4,387.86
5	1004	$85,616.00	5.00%	$4,280.80							
6	1005	$73,131.00	6.00%	$4,387.86							

Figure 2-6: An example of a transposed dataset.

In this example, the dataset on the left has been transposed to the range on the right. One of the cells in the transposed range has been selected to display the array function in the **Formula Bar** (as with all array functions and formulas, this function is exactly the same in all other cells in the transposed range). It is, technically speaking, a single function that exists in each cell in the range simultaneously. One other item of note is that the range on the right has been formatted to make it easier to compare to the original dataset on the left. However, the TRANSPOSE function does not carry formatting to the transposed range; you must reformat the new dataset yourself if you want the formatting to match.

> **Access the Checklist tile on your CHOICE Course screen for reference information and job aids on How to Use Lookup Functions.**

ACTIVITY 2-1
Using Lookup Functions

Data File
C:\091057Data\Using Lookup Functions and Formula Auditing\Employees.xlsx

Before You Begin
Excel 2016 is open.

Scenario
As a member of the Human Resources department, you have been given an employees workbook listing all employees. While you know several methods to find information about each employee, you decide to use Lookup functions to identify an employee's detail based on either what row in the list they are located or by their employee ID.

---

1. Open the **Employees.xlsx** workbook.
   a) In Excel, navigate to the **C:\091057Data\Using Lookup Functions and Formula Auditing** folder and open the workbook **Employees.xlsx**.
   b) Save the file as *My Employees.xlsx* in the **Using Lookup Functions and Formula Auditing** folder.

2. Identify the row that the employee record is located in the dataset using the MATCH function.
   a) Verify that the **Employees** worksheet is selected and enter *1001* in cell **B1**.
   b) Select cell **B2** and enter the formula *=MATCH(B1,A9:A59,0)*
   c) Verify that employee 1001 is found in row two of the dataset.

B2	▼	:	✕	✓	*fx*	=MATCH(B1,A9:A59,0)

◢	A	B	C
1	Employee ID	1001	
2	Row ID	2	

3. Find the employee name in the dataset based on the row ID using the INDEX function.
   a) Select cell **B3** and enter the formula *=INDEX(Data,B2,2)*

> 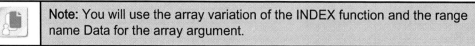 **Note:** You will use the array variation of the INDEX function and the range name Data for the array argument.

b) Verify that the employee name is Jacques Charon.

	A	B	C
	B3 ▼ : × ✓ *fx*	=INDEX(Data,B2,2)	
1	Employee ID	1001	
2	Row ID	2	
3	Employee	Charon, Jacques	

4. Find the employee's department using the VLOOKUP function based on the employee ID.

   a) Select cell **B4** and enter the formula *=VLOOKUP(B1,Data,3,FALSE)*
   b) Verify that the department identified for Jacques is Accounting.

	A	B	C
	B4 ▼ : × ✓ *fx*	=VLOOKUP(B1,Data,3,FAI	
1	Employee ID	1001	
2	Row ID	2	
3	Employee	Charon, Jacques	
4	Department	Accounting	

5. Identify the region of employee 1001.

   a) Select cell **B5** and enter the formula *=VLOOKUP(B1,Data,MATCH(A5,A9:F9,0),FALSE)*

   > **Note:** The MATCH function is nested within the VLOOKUP function.

   b) Verify that the region identified for Jacques is Southeast.

	A	B	C	D	E
	B5 ▼ : × ✓ *fx*	=VLOOKUP(B1,Data,MATCH(A5,A9:F9,0),FALSE)			
1	Employee ID	1001			
2	Row ID	2			
3	Employee	Charon, Jacques			
4	Department	Accounting			
5	Region	Southeast			

6. Identify the manager and extension of the employee.

   a) Select cell **B6** and enter the formula *=VLOOKUP(B1,Data,5,FALSE)*
   b) In cell **B7** enter the formula *=VLOOKUP(B1,Data,6,FALSE)*

c) Verify that Jacques' manager and extension is Marlon Pellham and 4459.

	A	B
1	Employee ID	1001
2	Row ID	2
3	Employee	Charon, Jacques
4	Department	Accounting
5	Region	Southeast
6	Manager	Pellham, Marlon
7	Extension	4459

7. Change the employee ID to identify the information for another employee.

   a) Select cell **B1** and enter *1046*
   b) Verify that all the employee information updates.

	A	B
1	Employee ID	1046
2	Row ID	47
3	Employee	Newton, Rosie
4	Department	Customer Service
5	Region	Southeast
6	Manager	Watson, Claire
7	Extension	4717

8. Save the workbook and keep the file open.

TOPIC B

Trace Cells

As users can introduce errors nearly anywhere within a workbook, tracking down errors is an important first step in resolving them. Additionally, errors aren't always obvious. Sometimes your only clue that a workbook contains an error at all is that some of the data on your worksheets doesn't seem to fit with surrounding figures. In these cases, you'll want to identify precisely which cells are feeding the erroneous data. That way, you can systematically check the data, formulas, or functions in only the cells that affect the erroneous result. But reading over the content in numerous cells to track which other cells feed into them can be a painstaking and error-prone process.

Fortunately, you don't always have to scour your worksheets, carefully examining each formula or function, to track down erroneous data feeding your formulas. Excel provides you with a clear, graphical method for determining precisely how the cells in your workbooks connect to one another: cell tracing. Taking advantage of this type of functionality will give you an instant snapshot of the relationships that exist in your workbooks. This means you won't have to painstakingly examine large, complex workbooks to isolate issues affecting your data and analysis.

Precedent and Dependent Cells

There are two basic types of relationships cells can have to one another: One cell can feed data into another cell, or it can be fed data by another cell. Cells that feed data into other cells are known as *precedent cells*. These cells precede other cells in a chain of relationships. A common example of precedent cells is a group of cells containing raw data that a function in some other cell adds together, as in the case of adding up a sales rep's quarterly sales to find his or her annual total. The cells that contain the raw quarterly sales figures are precedent cells that feed the function adding those figures up to return the annual total.

Cells that contain a formula or function that is fed by data in other cells are known as *dependent cells*. These cells depend on the data in other cells to perform some calculation. Continuing with the above example, the cell containing the function that adds up the quarterly sales figures is a dependent cell. Cells can be, and often are, both precedent and dependent cells simultaneously.

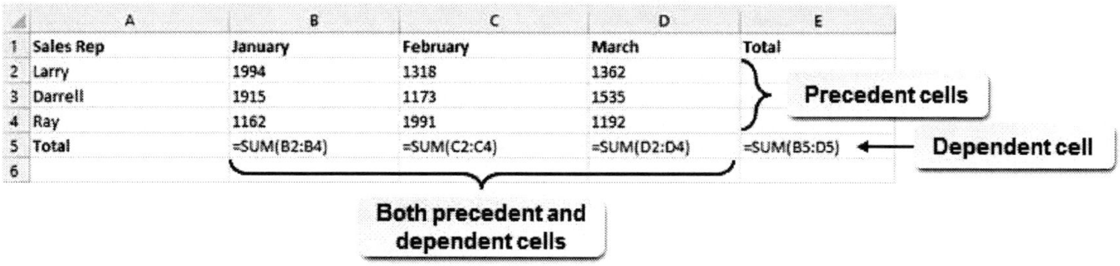

Figure 2-7: Precedent and dependent cells on an Excel worksheet.

> **Note:** This worksheet has formulas displayed instead of calculated values to illustrate the concepts of precedent and dependent cells.

The Trace Precedents and Trace Dependents Commands

You can use the **Trace Precedents** and **Trace Dependents** commands to graphically view the relationships among worksheet and workbook cells. When you select a cell and then select either of these commands, Excel displays one or more arrows on the worksheet that illustrate which cells either feed into or are fed by the selected cell. Although you can display these arrows for more than one cell simultaneously, you have to execute the commands for each cell one at a time.

You can trace more than one level of cell connectivity at a time by using these commands. The first time you select one of these commands with a cell selected, Excel displays arrows that trace the cell to the other cells that most directly relate to it. If you select one of these commands for a cell a second time, it traces either the precedent or the dependent cells one more level to display the cells that are feeding or fed by them, and so on. If the selected cell isn't related to other cells, Excel displays a message indicating this. You can access the **Trace Precedents** and **Trace Dependents** commands in the **Formula Auditing** group on the **Formulas** tab.

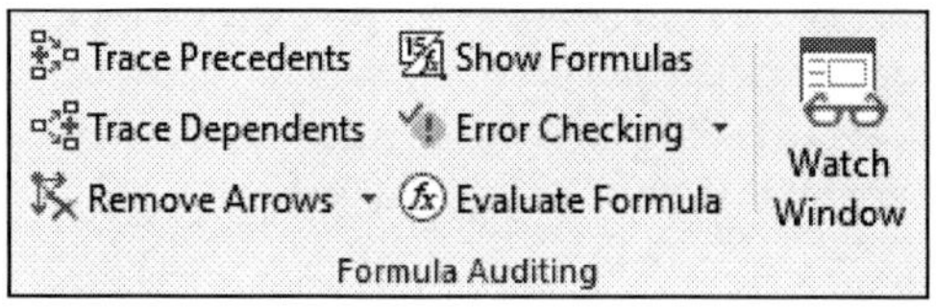

Figure 2-8: Use the Trace Precedents and Trace Dependents commands to view cell relationships.

Trace Arrows

The arrows that Excel displays when you execute either the **Trace Precedents** or the **Trace Dependents** command are called *trace arrows*. Trace arrows begin with a small dot, which indicates the precedent cell in the relationship, and end with an arrow, which indicates the dependent cell in the relationship. This is true regardless of which cell was traced.

Cells with more than one precedent or dependent cell will yield multiple trace arrows to show all first-level connections. There are three styles of trace arrows that each represent a different type of relationship: blue trace arrows, red trace arrows, and black, dashed-line trace arrows.

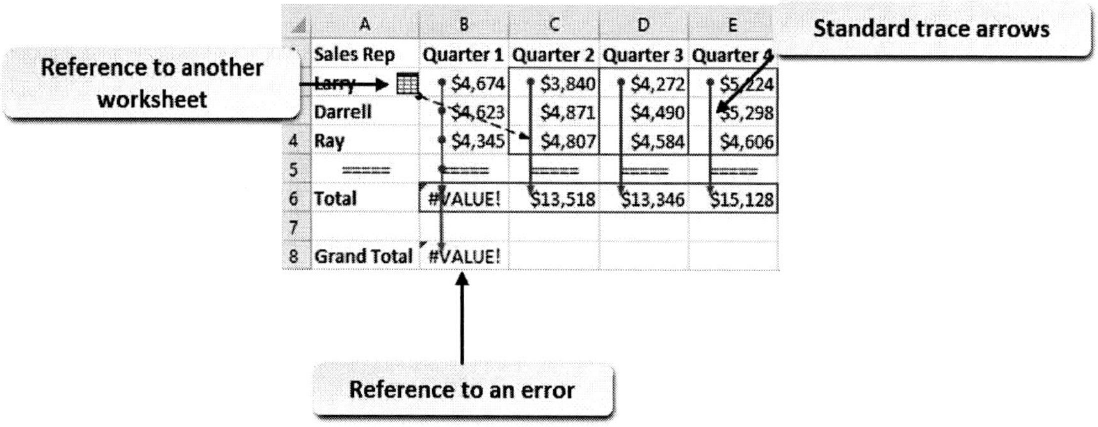

Figure 2-9: The various trace arrows not only display the direct relationships among cells, but they can also indicate links to other worksheets and workbooks, or formula errors.

The following table describes the three types of Excel trace arrows.

Trace Arrow Style	Traces
Blue arrow	Relationships of cells on the same worksheet.
Red arrow	Relationships of cells to other cells that contain formula or function errors.
Black, dashed-line arrow	Relationships of cells to other cells on different worksheets or in different workbooks.

> **Note:** Red trace arrows only indicate a relationship to a cell that contains an actual cell error, such as the #DIV/0! or #VALUE! errors. Excel will not display red trace arrows if the precedent or dependent cells contain invalid data due to data validation criteria, formulas or functions that are inconsistent with surrounding functions (or other errors that Excel flags by using the small, green triangle error indicator), or simply the wrong data.

The Go To Dialog Box and Trace Arrows

You can use the **Go To** dialog box to navigate to precedent or dependent cells on other worksheets to examine them and/or to correct errors in them. Excel displays the **Go To** dialog box when you double-click a black, dashed-line trace arrow. This is the same **Go To** dialog box that you can access on the ribbon by selecting **Home→Editing→Find & Select→Go To**. The only difference in its functionality in relation to trace arrows is that, when opened by double-clicking a black, dashed-line trace arrow, the **Go To** dialog box displays a list of all of the precedent or dependent cells on other worksheets that are connected to the cell you're tracing, enabling you to quickly navigate to any of them.

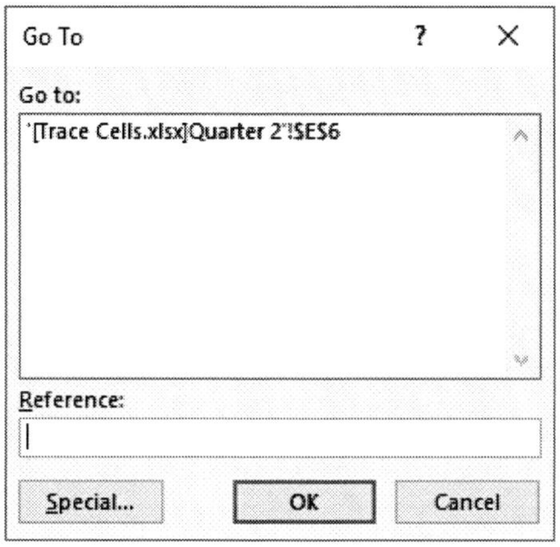

Figure 2-10: The Go To dialog box provides you with quick access to precedent and dependent cells.

> **Note:** If a precedent or dependent cell is on the same worksheet as the traced cell, but out of view due to scrolling or magnification, double-clicking a blue trace arrow navigates you to the associated related cell.

Go To Special Dialog Box

You can also use the **Go To Special** dialog box to navigate to precedents or dependents on the same worksheet. To access the **Go To Special** dialog box, select a cell that you wish to find the precedents for and on the ribbon, select **Home→Editing→Find & Select→Go To Special** and then select **Precedents**.

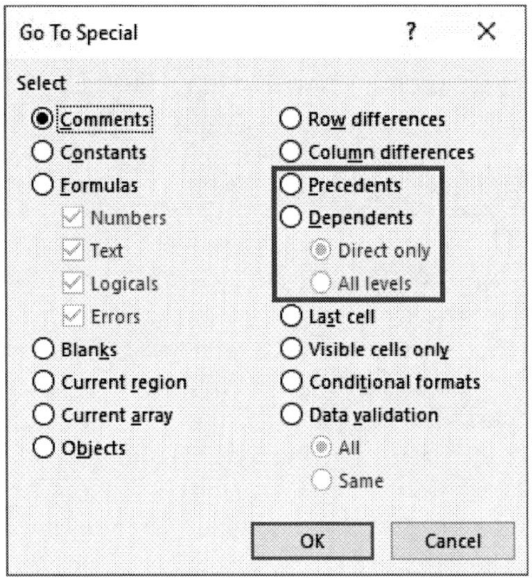

Figure 2-11: The Go To Special dialog box also provides access to precedent and dependent cells.

The Remove Arrows Options

Once you've identified the errors in your worksheet cells, you will likely want to remove trace arrows from view. Excel provides you with three different options for removing trace arrows, which you can access by selecting **Formulas→Formula Auditing→Remove Arrows drop-down arrow**.

Remove Arrows Option	Removes
Remove Arrows	All trace arrows from the currently selected worksheet. This option will not remove trace arrows from other worksheets.
Remove Precedent Arrows	All trace arrows from the currently selected cell to its precedent cells. This option will not remove trace arrows to dependent cells or any trace arrows from other worksheets.
Remove Dependent Arrows	All trace arrows from the currently selected cell to its dependent cells. This option will not remove trace arrows to precedent cells or any trace arrows from other worksheets.

 Access the Checklist tile on your CHOICE Course screen for reference information and job aids on How to Trace Precedent and Dependent Cells.

ACTIVITY 2-2
Tracing Precedent and Dependent Cells

Before You Begin
The My Employees.xlsx workbook is open.

Scenario
After entering the Lookup functions to identify any employees' details, you decide to use trace arrows to see how the functions retrieve the data. This also provides you with a visual representation that the functions are evaluating correctly.

---

1. Trace the precedents for various functions.

   a) Select cell **F2** and then select **Formulas→Formula Auditing→Trace Precedents**.
   b) Double-click the blue trace arrow.
   c) Observe that the cell **B4** is selected.
   d) Double-click the black, dashed-line arrow.

	A	B	C	D	E	F	G	H
1	Employee ID	1046				Average Department Salary		
2	Row ID	47				50,477.56		
3	Employee	Newton, Rosie						
4	Department	Customer Service						
5	Region	Southeast						
6	Manager	Watson, Claire						
7	Extension	4717						

   e) In the **Go To** dialog box, in the **Go to** section, select the second reference to **[My Employees.xlsx]Pay Data!$D$2:$D$51** and select **OK**.

   Go To   ?   X

   Go to:

   '[My Employees.xlsx]Pay Data'!$B$2:$B$51
   '[My Employees.xlsx]Pay Data'!$D$2:$D$51

   Reference:

   '[My Employees.xlsx]Pay Data'!$D$2:$D$51

   [Special...]   [OK]   [Cancel]

   f) Observe that the range of **D2:D51** is selected on the **Pay Data** worksheet.

2. Remove the precedent arrows.

---

a) Select the **Employees** worksheet and select cell **F2** and then select **Formulas→Formula Auditing→Remove Arrows drop-down arrow→Remove Precedent Arrows**.

3. Trace all dependents for the Employee ID.

a) Select cell **B1** and then select **Formulas→Formula Auditing→Trace Dependents**.
b) Select **Trace Dependents** again.
c) Observe that there are many formulas dependent on Employee ID.

	A	B	C	D	E	F	G	H
1	Employee ID	1046				Average Department Salary		
2	Row ID	47				$50,139.78		
3	Employee	Newton, Rosie						
4	Department	Customer Service						
5	Region	Southeast						
6	Manager	Watson, Claire						
7	Extension	4717						

d) Select **Remove Arrows drop-down arrow→Remove Dependent Arrows**.

4. Save the workbook and keep the file open.

TOPIC C

Watch and Evaluate Formulas

When you develop and work with workbooks that contain large numbers of complex functions or that have a lot of interconnected cells, it becomes tricky to fully troubleshoot and resolve all problems. For example, if the errors in a function are being caused by multiple cells throughout the workbook, it can become tedious to find the offending cells, resolve the issues in them, and then navigate back to the function to check to see if the change is reflected there. Or, you may encounter errors in highly complex functions with numerous levels of nesting and multiple other functions as arguments. In such complicated functions, it may not be immediately clear precisely what is causing the issue. It could be an error in entering a function or its arguments, an error in a precedent cell for any argument in any of the nested functions, or any number of other issues. At first glance, it could be nearly impossible to determine what part of the function is truly the problem.

Although you could painstakingly scour your worksheets to determine if the changes you're making reflect in all connected cells, or break down complex functions to determine precisely where an issue is coming from, you likely don't have that kind of time, and who would really want to do this anyway? Fortunately, Excel provides you with a couple of powerful tools that can help you watch formulas and their results and to break down complex functions argument-by-argument to home in on the issue. It's easy to see how this type of automated help can save you a ton of time, numerous headaches, and a lot of effort.

The Watch Window

Once you've found the cells containing the errors that you need to resolve, you want to be sure the changes you are making are actually taking effect in the dependent cells being fed by the errors. In many cases, this will be easy to do, as the cells may all be near each other on the same worksheet. But, what if the related cells are on opposite sides of a massive worksheet or are on different worksheets or in different workbooks entirely? Or, perhaps, you're correcting an error in a cell that is affecting formulas and functions in a number of different places. In these cases, you'll want a way to be able to watch the effects of correcting errors take place in the dependent cells regardless of where they are in a workbook. To do this, you can use the *Watch Window*.

The **Watch Window** is a floating pane that you can either move around the screen or dock within the Excel user interface above the **Formula Bar**. You can add any cells you want to watch to the **Watch Window**. For each cell you add to it, the **Watch Window** displays the cell's location, its displayed value, and, if it contains one, the formula or function entered into it. As you update the values or other formulas and functions in the precedent cells for cells in the **Watch Window**, the cell's information updates in real time. This ensures you don't have to navigate through or across workbooks to see the effects of updating information or correcting errors. You can access the **Watch Window** by selecting **Formulas→Formula Auditing→Watch Window**.

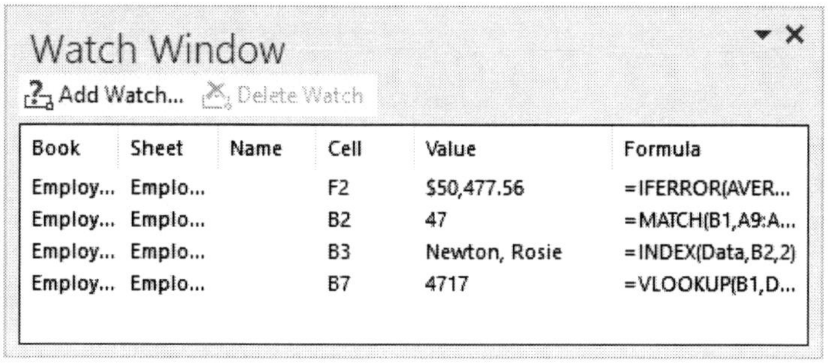

Book	Sheet	Name	Cell	Value	Formula
Employ...	Emplo...		F2	$50,477.56	=IFERROR(AVER...
Employ...	Emplo...		B2	47	=MATCH(B1,A9:A...
Employ...	Emplo...		B3	Newton, Rosie	=INDEX(Data,B2,2)
Employ...	Emplo...		B7	4717	=VLOOKUP(B1,D...

Figure 2-12: Use the Watch Window to instantly see updates to cells when you make changes to their precedent cells.

Formula Evaluation

When you need to correct errors in large, complex formulas or functions, it's helpful to break them down into their component parts (function arguments or elements of formula expressions) to examine each chunk by itself. This process is known as *formula evaluation*. Performing this type of task manually can be a painstaking, time-intensive process, but you don't have to do this manually. Excel 2016's Evaluate Formula feature can do this for you. When you evaluate a formula in Excel, Excel breaks the formula or function down into its component parts, runs the calculation on each part one at a time, and displays the result of that calculation to you in relation to the rest of the larger formula. This enables you to watch how Excel evaluates the formula to determine precisely where an error is taking place.

The Evaluate Formula feature evaluates the formula in the same order that Excel does when performing the calculation. In other words, it follows the order of operations just as Excel does when you first enter the formula. You can access the Evaluate Formula feature by selecting **Formulas→Formula Auditing→Evaluate Formula**.

The Evaluate Formula Dialog Box

When you run the Evaluate Formula feature on a formula or function, Excel opens it in the **Evaluate Formula** dialog box. When Excel first opens the **Evaluate Formula** dialog box, it displays the selected formula or function exactly as it is entered into the cell, and it underlines the first element of the formula or function that Excel would evaluate according to the order of operations. When you evaluate that element of the formula or function, Excel runs the calculation and changes the argument or calculation to the result of that argument or calculation. Excel then underlines the next element of the function or formula that it would normally evaluate. You can then ask Excel to perform that calculation, which will, in turn, display the result of it inline with its place in the larger formula. You continue this process until you have evaluated the entire formula or function, or until you have identified the cause of the issue.

Excel also provides you with the option to step in to the currently evaluated formula element to view information about where it's coming from. When you step in to an element of a formula or function, Excel opens a new text field in the **Evaluate Formula** dialog box. This field displays further information about that particular formula or function element. If that element is a hard-coded numeric value, it appears simply as the value. If the element is the result of a formula or function, the field displays the formula or function that produced the result, and so on.

 Note: Remember that Excel uses the order of operations or precedence to calculate formulas and functions. Formulas with parentheses and exponents are calculated first, then multiplication and division, and finally addition and subtraction.

Formula being evaluated

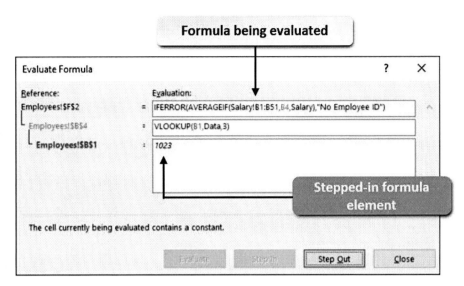

Stepped-in formula element

Figure 2-13: Use the Evaluate Formula dialog box to break complex formulas and functions down into component parts to examine how Excel is returning the result.

Access the Checklist tile on your CHOICE Course screen for reference information and job aids on How to Watch and Evaluate Formulas.

ACTIVITY 2-3
Watching and Evaluating Formulas

Before You Begin

The My Employees.xlsx workbook is open.

Scenario

After tracing the precedents and dependents of the various formulas, you wish to try out the **Watch Window** and to see how Excel evaluates the formulas you created. To see what happens, you decide to delete the Employee ID you entered earlier which will create errors in some of your formulas.

---

1. Add watches to several cells.

    a) Select **Formulas→Formula Auditing→Watch Window**.
    b) In the **Watch Window** dialog box, select **Add Watch**.
    c) In the **Add Watch** dialog box, in the **Select the cells that you would like to watch the value of** field, select cell **F2** and select **Add**.
    d) Select **Add Watch** again and select the range **B2:B7** and select **Add**.

2. Observe the changes to the **Watch Window** after deleting the Employee ID in cell B1.

    a) Select cell **B1** and press **Delete**.
    b) Observe that the **Watch Window** updates the values of the cells being watched.

    > **Note:** Remember that the **Watch Window** can be moved, sized, and docked to any side of the screen you wish.

    ## Watch Window

    [?] Add Watch...   [X] Delete Watch

Book	Sheet	Name	Cell	Value	Formula
My Em...	Emplo...		F2	No Employee ID	=IFERROR(AVER...
My Em...	Emplo...		B2	#N/A	=MATCH(B1,A9:A...
My Em...	Emplo...		B3	#N/A	=INDEX(Data,B2,2)
My Em...	Emplo...		B4	#N/A	=VLOOKUP(B1,D...
My Em...	Emplo...		B5	#N/A	=VLOOKUP(B1,D...
My Em...	Emplo...		B6	#N/A	=VLOOKUP(B1,D...
My Em...	Emplo...		B7	#N/A	=VLOOKUP(B1,D...

    c) Select cell **B1**, if necessary, and enter *1023*

---

d) Observe that the **Watch Window** updates the values of the cells being watched.

Book	Sheet	Name	Cell	Value	Formula
My Em...	Emplo...		F2	$50,139.78	=IFERROR(AVER...
My Em...	Emplo...		B2	24	=MATCH(B1,A9:A...
My Em...	Emplo...		B3	Obrien, Tony	=INDEX(Data,B2,2)
My Em...	Emplo...		B4	Customer Service	=VLOOKUP(B1,D...
My Em...	Emplo...		B5	West	=VLOOKUP(B1,D...
My Em...	Emplo...		B6	Watson, Claire	=VLOOKUP(B1,D...
My Em...	Emplo...		B7	4117	=VLOOKUP(B1,D...

e) Close the **Watch Window**.

3. **Evaluate the formula in cell F2.**

   a) Select cell **F2** and select **Formulas→Formula Auditing→Evaluate Formula**.
   b) In the **Evaluate Formula** dialog box, select **Step In**.
   c) Select **Evaluate** three times, observing the evaluation of the VLOOKUP function in cell **B4**.
   d) Select **Step Out**.
   e) Select **Evaluate** three times, observing the evaluation process of the outer function.
   f) Verify that the average department salary for Customer Services is $50,139.78.

Evaluate Formula	? ×
Reference:	**Evaluation:**
Employees!$F$2	= *$50,139.78*

   To show the result of the underlined expression, click Evaluate. The most recent result appears italicized.

   [Restart] [Step In] [Step Out] [Close]

   g) Select **Close**.

4. **Save and close the My Employees.xlsx workbook.**

Summary

In this lesson, you used various Lookup functions to find information from your worksheet data, you also learned how to audit your formulas by tracing precedent and dependent cells, as well as watching and evaluating formulas. You do not always need problems in your formulas to use these tools. Understanding their capabilities is beneficial as you learn to work with larger and larger workbooks and more and more complex formulas and functions, and they are extremely helpful when you do encounter problems. The more familiar you become with Excel's auditing features, the more quickly you'll be able to locate and fix issues in your workbooks.

How will incorporating Lookup functions into your workbooks affect your ability to analyze organizational data?

Can you think of a time when using Excel's auditing and evaluation functionality would have come in handy?

 Note: Check your CHOICE Course screen for opportunities to interact with your classmates, peers, and the larger CHOICE online community about the topics covered in this course or other topics you are interested in. From the Course screen you can also access available resources for a more continuous learning experience.

3 Sharing and Protecting Workbooks

Lesson Time: 1 hour, 15 minutes

Lesson Introduction

Nothing happens in a vacuum. It is a near certainty that you collaborate with a number of people in different roles fairly regularly. And it's likely that some of those people contribute to or review your work in a variety of capacities. As such, it's essential that you be able to collaborate with colleagues, provide and receive feedback on workbooks, and ensure that everyone's input is reflected in the final version of your documents. Unfortunately, the more you share and collaborate with others, especially when they have differing levels of authority or clearance, the more you need to ensure your critical organizational data is protected. But, how do you balance the need to share with the need to keep a wrap on your sensitive information?

Fortunately, Microsoft® Office Excel® 2016 includes a number of features and capabilities that enable you to navigate the fine balance between collaboration and security. Understanding how these features and capabilities work and how they work together will help you balance these concerns, keep your important work on track, and provide you with the peace of mind that comes with knowing your information is secure.

Lesson Objectives

In this lesson, you will share and protect workbooks. You will:

- Collaborate on a workbook.

- Protect worksheets and workbooks.

TOPIC A

Collaborate on a Workbook

It is likely that multiple people will have some degree of input on some of your workbooks. For example, you may be called upon to put together a sales report to present to management, but that report may have to be reviewed and approved by the sales manager first. Or, you may simply be part of a team responsible for performing some type of data analysis to present to other people in your organization. So, it's important that you be able to give and receive feedback on workbook files. Additionally, sharing workbook files back and forth via email or portable storage, ensuring that everyone who needs to contribute is able to, and keeping track of various versions to ensure that everyone's work is included can quickly become a nightmare. In short, you need a reliable method of sharing workbook files with a number of people while ensuring that the final version of that file actually includes the data it should.

Excel 2016 includes, and is compatible with, a number of features that enable you to collaborate on a wide scale while making sure nothing slips through the cracks. Taking advantage of this type of functionality enables you and your colleagues to work together smoothly, regardless of everyone's schedule or availability, while making sure the data and analysis you provide is complete, accurate, and up-to-date. With the volume of data that organizations generate, and the amount of change they nearly constantly face, this level of accuracy and efficiency is a must to stay competitive in today's market.

Comments

Comments are a type of worksheet markup that enable workbook users to convey information to one another. You can use comments to provide feedback during a review cycle or to provide other workbook users with additional information about the data a worksheet contains or the type of data they should be entering. Comments appear in a pop-up window that opens when you point the mouse pointer at a cell containing a comment. By default, cells containing comments display a red, triangular comment indicator in the top-right corner.

You can toggle the display of a single comment on or off, and you can toggle the display of all comments on or off simultaneously. You can also move and resize comment pop-up windows to better accommodate your view of either the comments or your worksheets. And, Excel enables you to navigate from comment to comment, so you can easily review all comments in large worksheets without having to hunt for them by scrolling. You can access the commands for working with comments in the **Comments** group on the **Review** tab.

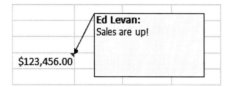

Figure 3–1: An open comment on an Excel worksheet.

 Note: You can update the user name that appears in a comment by setting the user name property in **Excel Options** on the **General** tab in the **Personalize your copy of Microsoft Office** section by selecting **File→Options**.

The following table describes the functions of the commands in the **Comments** group.

Comments Group Command	Use This To
New Comment/Edit Comment	Create a new comment in the currently selected cell or edit an existing comment in the currently selected cell.
Delete	Delete the comment in the currently selected cell.
Previous	Navigate to the previous comment in the workbook.
Next	Navigate to the next comment in the workbook.
Show/Hide Comment	Toggle the display of the comment in the currently selected cell on or off.
Show All Comments	Toggle the display of all comments in a workbook on or off.
Show Ink	Show or hide notation markup on a worksheet. This functionality is available only on tablets or other touchscreen devices, or if you open a file that was created on one of those devices.

Shared Workbooks

Excel 2016 provides you with the ability to collaborate with others on the same workbook in ways that go beyond providing simple feedback. By creating a *shared workbook*, you activate a host of features that enable multiple users to view and edit the same workbook. You can store a shared workbook in a central location, such as a Microsoft® SharePoint® site or an organizational network share. From there, multiple users can access and edit the workbook. If a SharePoint site or a network share aren't available, you can also distribute a shared workbook to multiple users, and then merge everyone's contributions in a master copy.

> **Note:** Working with shared workbooks on a SharePoint site or a network share is beyond the scope of this course. For more information on this functionality, visit **office.microsoft.com**.

Although shared workbooks provide you with powerful collaboration functionality, there are a number of Excel features that are not supported by shared workbooks. Perhaps the biggest downfall of shared workbooks is that they do not support tables at all. You have to convert tables back to ranges in order to create a shared workbook. Additionally, there are several features that can exist in a shared workbook but that users cannot change once the workbook is shared. Among these are merged cells, conditional formatting, charts, hyperlinks, subtotals, and PivotTable reports.

Figure 3-2: Shared workbooks display [Shared] after the workbook file name in the Title bar.

> **Note:** Sorting and filtering in shared workbooks can cause a number of data errors, especially when multiple users are trying to sort or filter at the same time. It is generally a good idea to discourage sorting and filtering in shared workbooks.

Change Tracking

Change tracking is a feature of shared workbooks that marks up particular worksheet elements whenever users make changes to the original content. If you turn on change tracking in a non-shared workbook, Excel converts it to a shared workbook. Tracked changes help you to easily identify modifications made to the document, identify precisely what change was made, and provide you with the ability to either accept or reject the changes. As with comments, when you place the mouse pointer over a cell containing tracked changes or over other change markup, Excel displays a pop-up window containing information about the specific change.

In addition to having Excel display changes as markup on your worksheets, you can set the change tracking feature to create a list of all changes on a separate worksheet within the workbook. When you enable this feature, Excel automatically creates a new worksheet titled **History** in the workbook, and generates a detailed log of all changes on it.

 Note: If you turn change tracking off, Excel deletes all markup and the record of what users have changed since you began tracking changes.

Change tracking affects some, but not all, changes made to your documents. Entering, modifying, and deleting cell data is tracked. So is adding or deleting rows or columns. But Excel does not track the following changes: cell formatting, hiding and unhiding rows or columns, and adding or revising comments. Other changes, such as revising worksheet names and inserting or deleting worksheets, are only tracked in the **History** worksheet, but not with markup.

Change tracking markup

	A	B	C
1	Region	Sales	
2	Southeast	15408	
3	West	18233	
4	Southwest	19434	
5	Northeast	15306	
6	Midwest	19565	
7			

Figure 3–3: Change tracking marks up most significant worksheet changes.

The Highlight Changes Dialog Box

You will use the **Highlight Changes** dialog box to enable change tracking and to configure change tracking options. To access the **Highlight Changes** dialog box, select **Review→Changes→Track Changes→Highlight Changes**.

Highlight Changes	? ✕
☑ Track changes while editing. This also shares your workbook.	
Highlight which changes	
☑ When:	Since I last saved ⌄
☐ Who:	Everyone ⌄
☐ Where:	▥
☑ Highlight changes on screen	
☐ List changes on a new sheet	
	OK Cancel

Figure 3–4: Use the Highlight Changes dialog box to specify how you want Excel to track changes to your workbooks.

The following table describes the functions of the various **Highlight Changes** dialog box elements.

Highlight Changes Dialog Box Element	Enables You To
Track changes while editing. This also shares your workbook. check box	Enable or disable change tracking.
When drop-down menu	Select which changes Excel will display based on when users make the changes. You can view all changes since you last saved the workbook, all changes made since a particular date, only changes you have not yet reviewed, or all changes since you enabled change tracking.
Who drop-down menu	Select which changes Excel will display based on who made the changes. You can view changes made by all users or all users except yourself.
Where field	Select the cells for which Excel will track changes. If you do not set a particular range for change tracking, Excel will track the entire workbook.
Highlight changes on screen check box	View tracked changes as on-screen markup.
List changes on a new sheet check box	View tracked changes in a log on a separate worksheet.

The Accept or Reject Changes Dialog Boxes

There are two dialog boxes you will use to either accept or reject the tracked changes in your workbooks: the **Select Changes to Accept or Reject** dialog box and the **Accept or Reject Changes** dialog box. You will use the **Select Changes to Accept or Reject** dialog box to choose which changes to accept or reject based on when they were made, who made them, and where they appear in the worksheet. These options are essentially the same as those available in the **Highlight Changes** dialog box. Think of this as filtering down all of the changes made in your workbooks so that you can then decide which specific changes to keep or discard. To start the process of accepting or rejecting changes, select **Review→Changes→Track Changes drop-down arrow→Accept/ Reject Changes**.

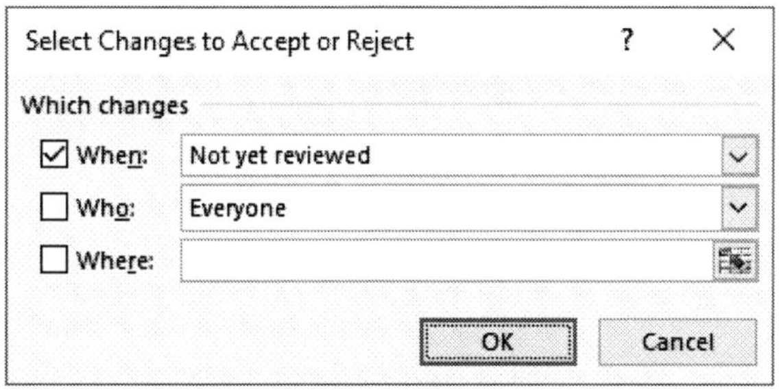

Figure 3-5: The Select Changes to Accept or Reject dialog box.

Once you have selected the desired options in the **Select Changes to Accept or Reject** dialog box, you will use the **Accept or Reject Changes** dialog box to choose whether or not to keep the specific changes users have made to your workbooks, either one at a time or all at once. The **Accept or Reject Changes** dialog box displays information about the currently selected change, such as who made the change, when it was made, and the particular details about the change. As each change appears in the **Change X of Y made to this document** section, you can choose to accept or reject the change individually, or you can choose to accept or reject all changes you included when configuring options in the **Select Changes to Accept or Reject** dialog box simultaneously.

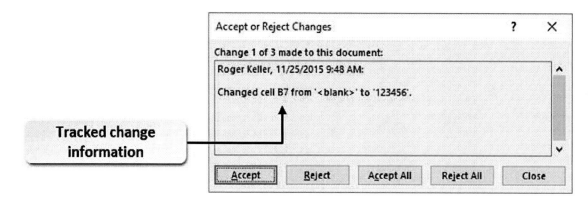

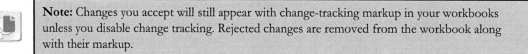

Figure 3-6: The Accept or Reject Changes dialog box.

Note: Changes you accept will still appear with change-tracking markup in your workbooks unless you disable change tracking. Rejected changes are removed from the workbook along with their markup.

The Compare and Merge Workbooks Command

If you are collaboratively working on a shared workbook that is not saved in a central location, such as a SharePoint site or a network share, you will still need to include the work other users contribute in the master copy of the workbook. To do this, you use the **Compare and Merge Workbooks Command**. This Excel feature enables you to merge two or more copies of the same shared workbook into a single file. When you select the **Compare and Merge Workbooks Command**, Excel opens the **Select Files to Merge Into Current Workbook** dialog box, which allows you to select one or more other workbook files to merge with the currently selected workbook file.

Important considerations to keep in mind when using this feature include:

- All workbooks that you wish to merge must be copies of the original shared workbook with unique file names and be stored in the same folder/directory.
- You cannot choose which changes to accept and which changes to reject when merging workbooks.
- Excel gives priority to the most recently merged workbook when there are conflicts between changes. If you merge more than one workbook into the master copy simultaneously, the one that appears last in the **Select Files to Merge Into Current Workbook** dialog box is given priority.
- If you have change tracking enabled in the master copy, Excel flags the changes in the markup or the change history.
- The **Compare and Merge Workbooks Command** does not appear on the ribbon or the **Quick Access Toolbar** by default. You must add that as a customization.

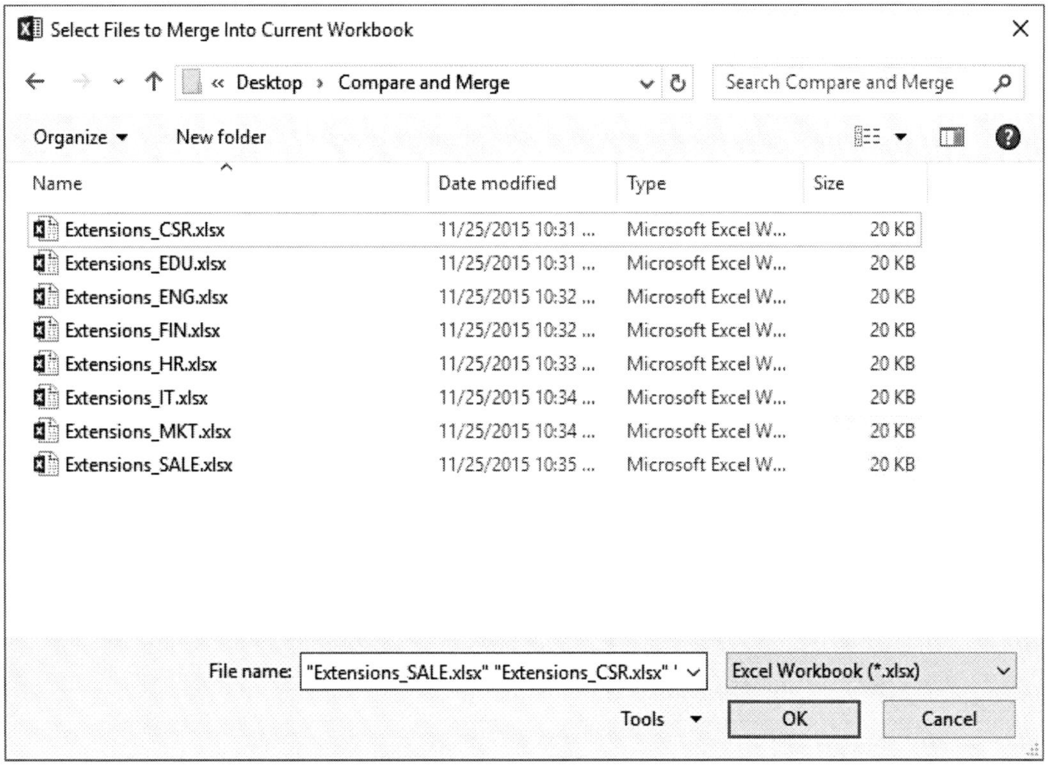

X Select Files to Merge Into Current Workbook				✕

← → ∨ ↑	« Desktop › Compare and Merge	∨ ↻	Search Compare and Merge ⌕

Organize ▾   New folder

Name	Date modified	Type	Size
X Extensions_CSR.xlsx	11/25/2015 10:31 ...	Microsoft Excel W...	20 KB
X Extensions_EDU.xlsx	11/25/2015 10:31 ...	Microsoft Excel W...	20 KB
X Extensions_ENG.xlsx	11/25/2015 10:32 ...	Microsoft Excel W...	20 KB
X Extensions_FIN.xlsx	11/25/2015 10:32 ...	Microsoft Excel W...	20 KB
X Extensions_HR.xlsx	11/25/2015 10:33 ...	Microsoft Excel W...	20 KB
X Extensions_IT.xlsx	11/25/2015 10:34 ...	Microsoft Excel W...	20 KB
X Extensions_MKT.xlsx	11/25/2015 10:34 ...	Microsoft Excel W...	20 KB
X Extensions_SALE.xlsx	11/25/2015 10:35 ...	Microsoft Excel W...	20 KB

File name: "Extensions_SALE.xlsx" "Extensions_CSR.xlsx" ' ∨   Excel Workbook (*.xlsx) ∨

Tools ▾   OK   Cancel

Figure 3-7: Copies of a workbook that can be merged with the original.

The Share Options

As you won't always need or be able to share Excel workbooks via SharePoint or a network share, you'll want to have other options for collaborating on and distributing workbooks. Excel 2016 provides you with a variety of options for doing so. You can access these options on the **Share** tab in the **Backstage** view.

Share

Sharing and Protecting Workbooks
Desktop

Share

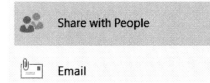
Share with People

Email

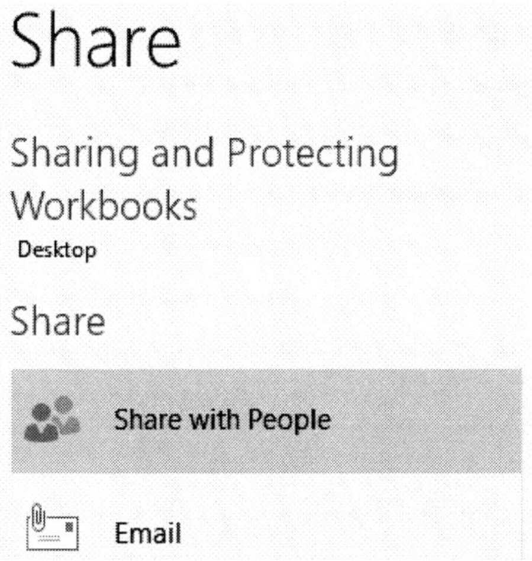

Figure 3-8: The file sharing options available in Excel's Backstage view.

 Note: It is important to note that files you share using the options on the **Share** tab in the **Backstage** view are not the same as shared workbooks. Functionality like change tracking and the Compare and Merge feature are not automatically included in workbooks you share via Microsoft® OneDrive® through these share options.

The following table describes the various Share options in Excel 2016.

Share Option	Enables You To
Share with People	Invite other users to view or edit Excel workbooks that you have saved to OneDrive.
Email	Attach copies of your workbooks in a number of file formats to email messages. You can also create links to include in email messages to workbooks you have saved to OneDrive. You must have an email client configured on your computer to use this feature.

Microsoft Accounts and OneDrive

Microsoft OneDrive is an online file storage, management, and sharing service that you can use to store, share, and collaborate on your Excel workbook files and other files. To use this service, you must sign up for a Microsoft account. If you already use one of Microsoft's other online services, such as the Outlook® (previously Hotmail) email service or Xbox Live®, you already have a Microsoft account.

 Note: There are two versions on OneDrive, personal and business. Anyone can create a personal OneDrive account but your organization would provide you the credentials for a business account.

One of the key benefits of OneDrive, in addition to the collaboration features, is that it enables you to access and work with your files from nearly any location on any number of devices. You can use either a web-based version of OneDrive or one of the OneDrive apps designed for a variety of platforms. Excel 2016 even includes built-in functionality that enables you to sign in to your Microsoft account to save, share, and access your workbook files from within the Excel application. Once you have signed in to your OneDrive account from within Excel 2016, you can access OneDrive from within Excel 2016 by selecting **File→Open**, and then selecting your OneDrive account. Likewise, you can save files to your OneDrive account by selecting **File→Save As**, and then selecting your OneDrive account. Signing in to your Microsoft account through Excel 2016 also activates some of Excel's collaboration features, which you would otherwise not have access to.

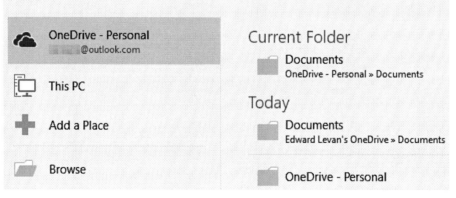

Figure 3-9: You can directly access your OneDrive account from within Excel in the Backstage view.

Excel Online

Some people with whom you share your workbook files may not have Excel installed on their computers. And, even if users do have Excel installed on their machines, they may not always have the computer with Excel on hand when they need to view or edit the documents you shared with them. In cases such as these, Microsoft offers an alternative to viewing and working with Excel workbook files in the Excel application: *Excel Online*. Excel Online is a scaled-down version of Excel that is available via an Internet connection through your web browser. You can use Excel Online to view and work with files you have saved in OneDrive, or workbook files that other users have shared with you via OneDrive.

> **Note:** There are two other similar, remote-based versions of Excel that you may encounter depending on your organization's particular network resources and how you access Excel: Excel Services and the Excel Web App. While these are largely similar versions of Excel, there are important differences. For more information on these other Excel services, visit **office.microsoft.com**.

One of the most significant differences between using the Excel application and using Excel Online is that files you work on using Excel Online automatically save as you work in them. This is because when sharing files via OneDrive, all users who have editing permissions are working on the same file, so it is important that all changes be updated for all users immediately. Additionally, several features available in the standard Excel application are not available via, or fully compatible with, Excel Online. These include certain form controls, data connections, data validation, and worksheet protection.

When you work with a file in Excel Online, you can view a list of all other users who are currently working on the file. Any changes they make to the file appear in near real time on your screen. However, if someone has the workbook file open in the standard Excel application, the file is locked for editing and cannot be edited using Excel Online. You can, however, view a read-only copy of the file or save a copy locally in such cases.

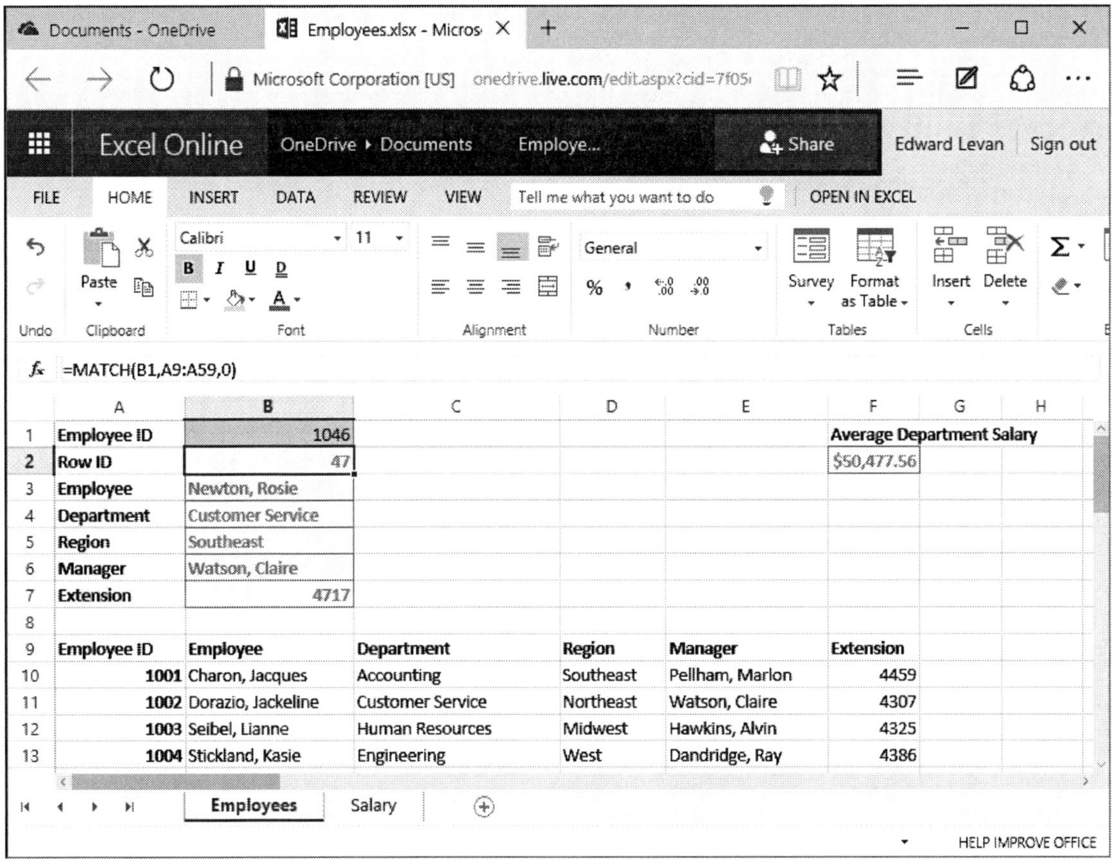

Figure 3-10: A workbook open in Excel Online.

The PDF and XPS File Formats

Not everyone you need to share your workbook files with will always have Excel installed on their computers or have immediate access to a computer that has Excel. As people use different versions of Excel, there are sometimes compatibility issues between files and Excel versions. And you may still need your data and your workbooks to display the precise formatting and layout you worked so hard to configure in the first place. Excel provides you with the ability to publish your Excel workbooks in two particular file formats that are well-suited to this need: the PDF and the XPS file formats.

PDF stands for Portable Document Format. This is an open standard for exchanging electronic documents that was developed by the Adobe® Corporation. Its file extension is .pdf. XPS stands for XML Paper Specification. This is a non-editable file format developed by Microsoft that you can generate from a number of programs, but that you can only view, sign, or set permissions for in Microsoft's XPS Viewer application. The XPS file format's file extension is .xps.

 Note: You can access the **Adobe Downloads** page from **www.adobe.com** to download the free Adobe® Reader® application. You can download the free XPS Viewer application from the Download Center at **www.microsoft.com**.

These file formats allow you to easily print or distribute workbooks regardless of whether or not document recipients have access to Excel, and they give you the peace of mind of knowing your documents will appear precisely as you configured them when opened. Additionally, the PDF file format enables your workbooks to be printed by commercial printers. You can publish your workbook files to either of these two formats by selecting **File→Export→Create PDF/XPS Document**, as well as share them via email by selecting **File→Share→Email** and then selecting the desired email sharing options.

Accessibility

If you will be sharing Excel workbooks, via any method, with other users who have some type of physical disability, you will want to ensure they can access all of the information included in your workbooks. And, if you work for a federal agency, section 508 of the U.S. Rehabilitation Act of 1973 requires that all of your electronic documents be accessible to people with disabilities (you may hear this referred to as being "508 compliant").

Fortunately, Excel 2016 includes several options that enable you to make your workbook files more accessible to persons with disabilities. And, there are some general guidelines you can follow when creating certain workbook elements that can make it easier for people with particular disabilities to more easily navigate, view, and work in your workbook files. The following table identifies and describes the accessibility options and guidelines that are pertinent to Excel 2016.

Accessibility Option	Description
Alternative text for objects and images	Adding alternative text to objects, such as images, charts, SmartArt graphics, and tables, enables people who use screen readers to access information about objects they aren't able to see. Alternative text, also known as alt text, provides a description of images and other objects to provide users with some context to understand what images and objects are in your workbooks and what their purpose is.
Clear column header information in tables	In addition to including alt text to describe your tables, you should also ensure that you format your tables to include headers (column labels) and ensure that those headers provide meaningful context about the information in the columns. This enables users who use screen readers to discern key information about the data in your tables and to more easily navigate to the desired information.

Accessibility Option	Description
Meaningful hyperlink text	You should ensure that hyperlink text in your workbooks provides a clear description of what hyperlinks link to. A simple example of this would be to use the text "Click here to open the annual report" instead of simply using a file path or URL as the hyperlink text.
Eliminating empty cells in datasets	You should avoid using blank cells, rows, or columns to differentiate among or separate content in your tables and data ranges. This helps users with screen readers as they are less likely to falsely believe they have reached the end of a dataset if it contains no empty cells.
Unique tab names and no blank worksheets	Giving all worksheet tabs meaningful names and deleting blank worksheets makes navigating workbooks easier for people with ambulatory issues and users who need screen readers.
Closed captioning	If you include audio or video assets in your workbook files, you should ensure that those files include captioning for users with hearing impairments.

The Accessibility Checker

The **Accessibility Checker** is an Excel 2016 task pane that enables you to inspect your workbook files for possible accessibility issues. If your workbook contains elements that might make it difficult for users with disabilities to fully understand its contents, the **Accessibility Checker** flags those elements as accessibility issues. The **Accessibility Checker** categorizes these elements into three different groups—errors, warnings, and tips—depending on the severity of the inaccessibility. You can access the **Accessibility Checker** by selecting **File→Info→Check for Issues→Check Accessibility**.

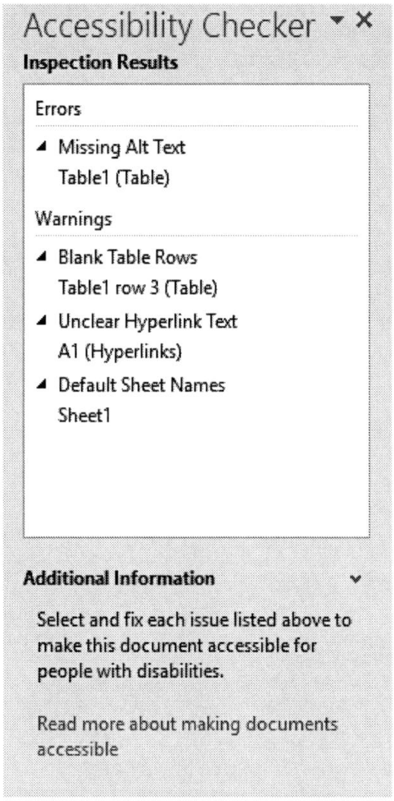

Accessibility Checker ▾ ✕

Inspection Results

Errors

◢ Missing Alt Text
  Table1 (Table)

Warnings

◢ Blank Table Rows
  Table1 row 3 (Table)
◢ Unclear Hyperlink Text
  A1 (Hyperlinks)
◢ Default Sheet Names
  Sheet1

Additional Information   ⌄

Select and fix each issue listed above to make this document accessible for people with disabilities.

Read more about making documents accessible

Figure 3-11: The Accessibility Checker with flagged issues.

The following table describes the three categories of accessibility issues.

Accessibility Issue Category	Describes Content That
Errors	Makes a workbook very difficult or impossible for people with disabilities to understand.
Warnings	In most cases, makes a workbook difficult for people with disabilities to understand.
Tips	People with disabilities can understand, but to improve their experience could be arranged or presented in a better way.

📋 Access the Checklist tile on your CHOICE Course screen for reference information and job aids on How to Collaborate on a Workbook.

ACTIVITY 3-1
Collaborating on a Workbook

Data Files

C:\091057Data\Sharing and Protecting Workbooks\Regional Salaries.xlsx

C:\091057Data\Sharing and Protecting Workbooks\Extensions.xlsx

C:\091057Data\Sharing and Protecting Workbooks\Extensions_ACC.xlsx

C:\091057Data\Sharing and Protecting Workbooks\Extensions_CSR.xlsx

C:\091057Data\Sharing and Protecting Workbooks\Extensions_EDU.xlsx

C:\091057Data\Sharing and Protecting Workbooks\Extensions_ENG.xlsx

Before You Begin

Excel 2016 is open.

Scenario

As a member of the Human Resources department, you have been given workbooks listing employees salaries by region and one with phone extensions by department. Your manager has asked you to track changes in the salary workbook so they can be approved. You also need some help completing the phone extensions in the list and have decided the best way to fill in all the extensions is to collaborate with the managers of each of the departments. You decide to add a comment indicating what is needed from each of the managers and fill in as much of the information as you know. This workbook has been shared with the other departments and you will need to track, compare, and merge the changes into your master workbook copy.

 Note: To save time in this activity, departmental copies of the master Extensions workbook were shared with the other departments and all the extensions have been entered.

1. Open the **Regional Salaries.xlsx** workbook.
   a) In Excel, navigate to C:\091057Data\Sharing and Protecting Workbooks folder and open the workbook **Regional Salaries.xlsx**.
   b) Save the file as **My Regional Salaries.xlsx** in the **Sharing and Protecting Workbooks** folder.

2. Insert a comment notifying users of what is in the workbook.
   a) Verify that the **Summary** worksheet is selected.
   b) Select cell **B1** and choose **Review→Comments→New Comment**.

    Note: You may also right-click cell **B1** and choose **Insert Comment**.

   c) Type *Average regional salaries are calculated here.*
   d) Select any other cell.

    e) Hover over cell **B1** and verify the comment appears.

B	C	D	E
Average Salary	**Ed Levan:** Average regional salaries are calculated here.		

    f) Save the workbook.

3. **Enable change tracking in the workbook.**

    a) Select **Review→Changes→Track Changes→Highlight Changes**.

    b) Select the check box **Track changes while editing. This also shares your workbook.**

    c) Verify that the **When** and **Highlight changes on screen** check boxes are selected and then select **OK**.

    d) In the **Microsoft Excel** dialog box indicating that this action will now save the workbook, select **OK**.

    e) Verify that [Shared] appears on the **Title bar** to the right of the file name.

4. **Pretend you are the manager for the Midwest region and that several employees have received salary increases that you need to update.**

    a) Select the **Midwest** worksheet.

    b) Update the following employee salaries.

      • **B2**: 72,500

      • **B3**: 77,500

      • **B11**: 70,500

c) Verify that the change tracking markup appears.

▲	A	B
1	Rep	Salary
2	E1110	$72,500
3	E1111	$77,500
4	E1112	$77,198
5	E1113	$65,105
6	E1114	$57,275
7	E1115	$82,168
8	E1116	$47,177
9	E1117	$62,778
10	E1118	$69,146
11	E1119	$70,500

d) Save the workbook.

5. Once again, as a member of the Human Resources department, accept the changes made to the workbook.

   a) Select **Review→Changes→Track Changes→Accept/Reject Changes**.
   b) In the **Select Changes to Accept or Reject** dialog box, select the **Who** check box and verify that **Everyone** is selected and select **OK**.
   c) In the **Accept or Reject Changes** dialog box for change 1 of 3, select **Accept**.
   d) In the **Accept or Reject Changes** dialog box, select **Accept All**.

6. Disable Highlight Changes and sharing of the workbook.

   a) Select **Review→Changes→Track Changes→Highlight Changes**.
   b) In the **Highlight Changes** dialog box, uncheck the **Track changes while editing. This also shares your workbook.** check box and select **OK**.
   c) In the **Microsoft Excel** dialog box indicating that this action will remove the workbook from shared use, select **Yes**.
   d) Verify that [Shared] has been removed from the **Title bar**.
   e) Save the file and keep the workbook open.

7. Open the master Extensions workbook.

   a) In Excel, open the workbook **Extensions.xlsx** and maximize the window if necessary.
   b) Observe that [Shared] appears on the **Title bar** after the file name.
   c) Observe that the extensions for Accounting, Customer Service, Education, and Engineering are not entered.

8. Enable the **Compare and Merge Workbooks** command on the **Quick Access Toolbar**.

   > Note: Since **Compare and Merge Workbooks** is not accessible from the ribbon, adding this command to the **Quick Access Toolbar** is necessary to complete this activity.

   a) Right-click the ribbon and select **Customize Quick Access Toolbar**.
   b) In the **Excel Options** window, from the **Choose commands from** drop-down arrow, select **All Commands**.
   c) From the commands list, select **Compare and Merge Workbooks** and select the **Add** button.
   d) In the **Excel Options** window, select **OK**.

9. Merge the files from the other departments into your master copy.

   a) On the **Quick Access Toolbar**, select **Compare and Merge Workbooks**.

b) Select the other **Extensions_XXX.xlsx** workbooks (refer to the image below), and select **OK**.

c) Observe that the remaining extensions have been added for the Accounting, Customer Service, Education, and Engineering departments.

	A	B	C
1	**Department**	**Employee**	**Extension**
2	Accounting	Edward	4991
3	Accounting	Crystal	4989
4	Accounting	Phoebe	1981
5	Accounting	Aaron	4980
6	Accounting	Melinda	4977
7	Customer Service	Herbert	4974
8	Customer Service	Craig	4971
9	Customer Service	Daryl	4970
10	Customer Service	Randal	4969
11	Customer Service	John	4966
12	Education	Peter	4965
13	Education	Jessica	4963
14	Engineering	Adrian	4962
15	Engineering	Thomas	4961
16	Engineering	James	4960

d) Save the workbook as **My Extensions.xlsx** in the **Sharing and Protecting Workbooks** folder.

10. Accept the changes made to the master Extensions workbook.

a) Select **Review→Changes→Track Changes→Accept/Reject Changes**.

b) In the **Select Changes to Accept or Reject** dialog box, select the **Who** check box and verify that **Everyone** is selected and select **OK**.

c) In the **Accept or Reject Changes** dialog box for change 1 of 15, select **Accept**.

d) In the **Accept or Reject Changes** dialog box, select **Accept All**.

11. Save the workbook in PDF format.

a) Select **File→Export→Create PDF/XPS Document→Create PDF/XPS**.

> 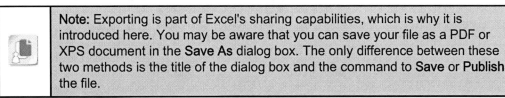 **Note:** Exporting is part of Excel's sharing capabilities, which is why it is introduced here. You may be aware that you can save your file as a PDF or XPS document in the **Save As** dialog box. The only difference between these two methods is the title of the dialog box and the command to **Save** or **Publish** the file.

b) In the **Publish as PDF or XPS** dialog box verify that the **Save as type** selected is **PDF (*.pdf)** and select **Publish**.

X📄 Publish as PDF or XPS	✕

← → · ↑ 📁 « Desk… › Sharing and Protecting Workbo…   ⌄ 🔄 | Search Sharing and Protectin… 🔎

Organize ▼   New folder   ▤▤ ▼   ❓

Name ˄	Date modified	Type	Size

No items match your search.

File name: My Extensions.pdf   ⌄

Save as type: PDF (*.pdf)   ⌄

☑ Open file after publishing   Optimize for: ⦿ Standard (publishing online and printing)

　　　　　　　　　　　　　　　　　　　○ Minimum size (publishing online)

　　　　　　　　　　　　　　　　　　　[Options...]

⏶ Hide Folders   Tools ▼   [Publish]   [Cancel]

> 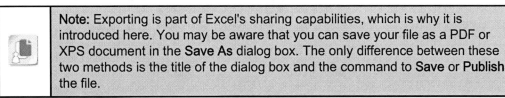 **Note:** If you see the **How do you want to open this file?** dialog box, you can select **Edge** to open the PDF if you don't have a program associated to open the PDF file.

c) Close the window displaying the PDF file.

12. Close the **My Extensions.xlsx** workbook and keep the **My Regional Salaries.xlsx** workbook open.

TOPIC B

Protect Worksheets and Workbooks

As you share your workbooks with more and more people, or as you collaborate on workbook files with others, you face an increased risk of someone accessing, modifying, or deleting your data without authorization. Collaboration is essential, but it is critical that you be able to ensure the integrity and the security of your organization's sensitive data. Whether by accident or by malicious action, damage to your data or the acquisition of your data by unauthorized parties can have serious negative implications for your organization. As such, it is critical that you be able to balance the need to gather input and share information with the need to keep sensitive information safe and intact.

Fortunately, Excel 2016 provides you with a number of options for protecting your worksheets and workbooks from unauthorized access or changes. Taking the time to fully understand these security features means you'll be able to include everyone who needs access to your Excel workbooks without worrying about the integrity or the security of your information.

Worksheet and Workbook Element Protection

There are two general levels at which you can protect elements of your Excel files: the workbook level and the worksheet level. Workbook protection always applies to the entire workbook. At the workbook level, Excel enables you to prevent users from adding or deleting worksheets, renaming or formatting worksheets, and viewing hidden worksheets.

At the worksheet level, Excel provides you with a number of options for allowing or preventing users from interacting with your data. For example, you can lock cells so they can't be edited, or you can hide cell formulas so that document recipients can view formula or function results only. You can also enable or disable such operations as formatting cells, columns, and rows; inserting or deleting columns and rows; sorting and filtering; and interacting with PivotTables.

Worksheet-level protection works hand-in-hand with cell protection formatting, which you apply by using the options on the **Protection** tab of the **Format Cells** dialog box. From there, you control whether or not cells on protected worksheets are locked and whether or not users can view formulas and functions. Keep in mind that these options apply only once you enable worksheet protection. By default, all worksheet cells are locked, so unless you manually change this setting for cells, all cells on protected worksheets are locked.

At either the workbook or the worksheet level, you can set a required password for users to be able to edit protected elements. Users with whom you have shared the password will be able to disable protection. If you do not set a password, no users will be able to edit the protected elements as long as the protection is enabled. However, if you don't require a password, other users will be able to disable workbook and worksheet protection. As this is the case, not setting a password is best suited to preventing accidental, not malicious, modifications.

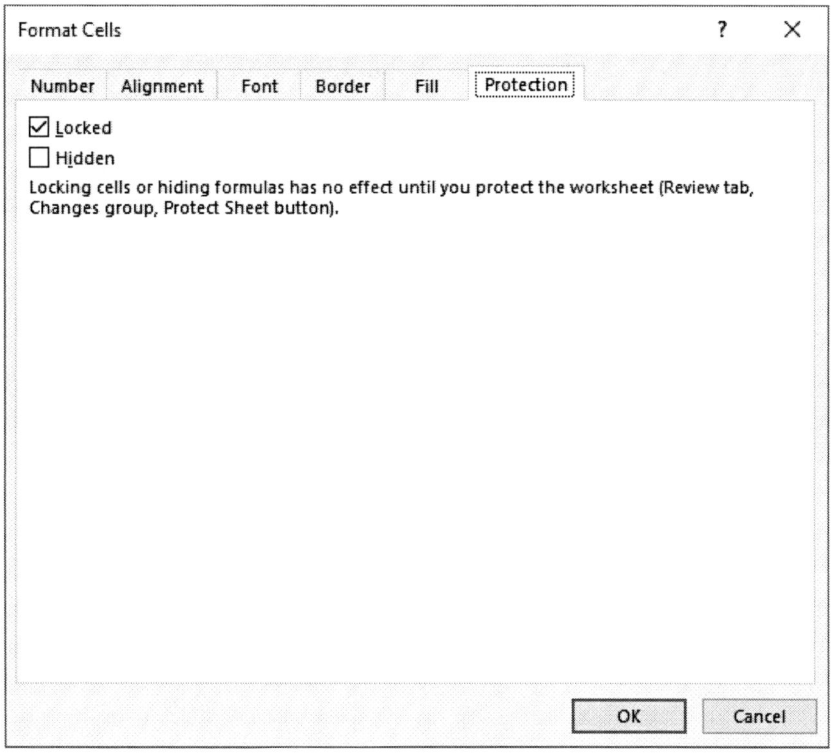

Figure 3-12: The cell protection formatting options become active once you enable worksheet protection.

The Protect Sheet Command

The **Protect Sheet** command opens the **Protect Sheet** dialog box, which enables you to select which actions workbook recipients are able to perform on a particular worksheet, set a required password for editing protected elements, and enable cell protection formatting. If you require a password for editing protected elements, you must remember the password or you will not be able to remove the protection. You can access the **Protect Sheet** dialog box by selecting **Review→Changes→Protect Sheet**.

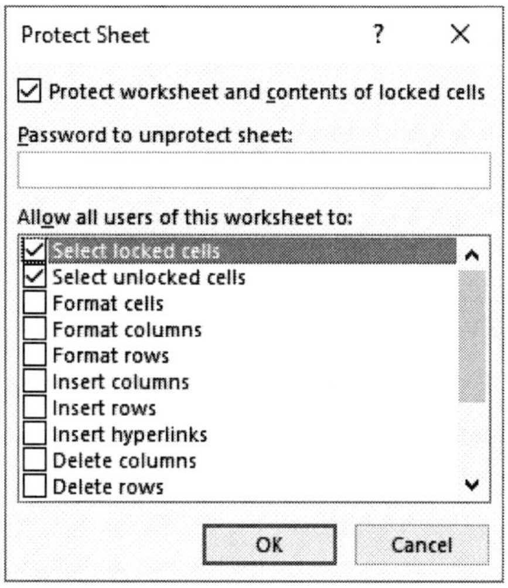

Figure 3-13: You can determine which worksheet elements users are able to edit by checking options in the Protect Sheet dialog box.

The Protect Workbook Command

The **Protect Workbook** command opens the **Protect Structure and Windows** dialog box, which you can use to enable or disable workbook-level protection and to require a password to disable workbook-level protection. In Excel 2016, the **Windows** check box is grayed out as the Excel UI no longer supports multiple open workbook windows within the same instance of the Excel user interface.

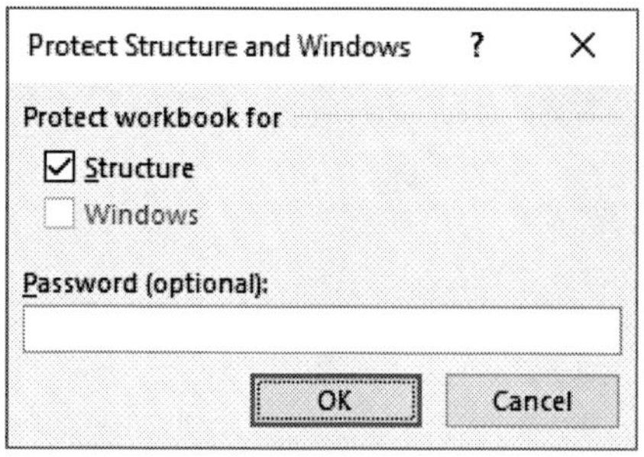

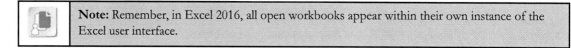

Figure 3-14: The Protect Structure and Windows dialog box.

Note: Remember, in Excel 2016, all open workbooks appear within their own instance of the Excel user interface.

The Protect Workbook Options

Protecting elements of your workbook may be sufficient to prevent accidental or intentional changes to your worksheet data, but there are several reasons you may want to add another layer of protection. For example, you may have workbooks that contain such highly sensitive data that you don't want anyone without specific permission or authority to even be able to open and view them. In these types of cases, you'll want to add overall workbook file-level security to your Excel files.

Excel 2016 provides you with a number of options for protecting your workbook files from unauthorized access. You can access and apply these options by selecting **File→Info→Protect Workbook**.

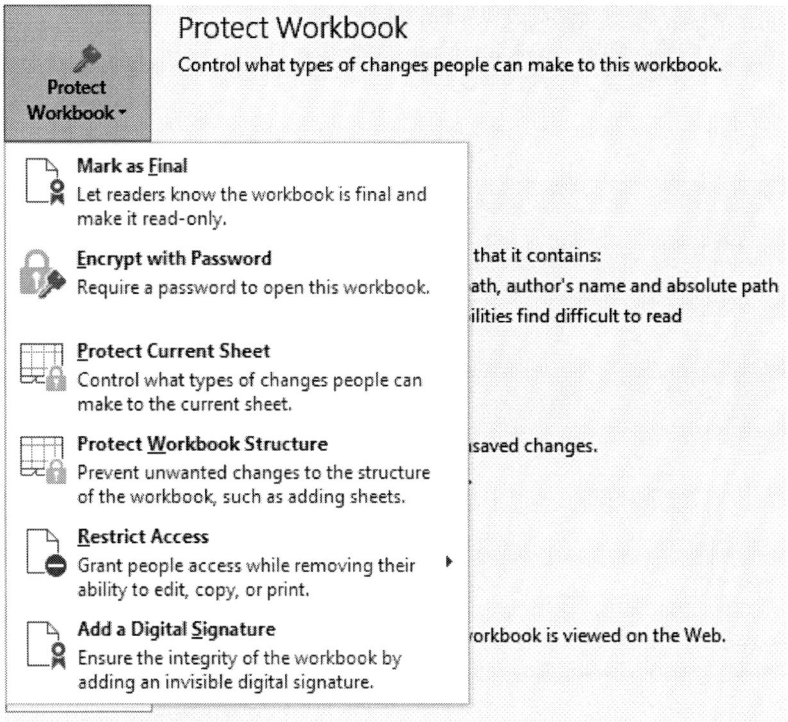

Figure 3-15: The Protect Workbook options in the Backstage view.

The following table describes the various **Protect Workbook** options.

Protect Workbook Option	Description
Mark as Final	Setting this option saves the workbook in Read Only mode, which disables editing commands and turns off proofing markup. When a workbook is in Read Only mode, the file name in the **Title bar** is appended with the text *[Read Only]*. It is important to understand that any user can revert a workbook back to an active state by either selecting the **Edit Anyway** button in the message bar upon opening the file, or by selecting **File→Info→Protect Workbook→Mark as Final**. This option protects only against accidental revisions.
Encrypt with Password	This option enables you to require any workbook user to enter a password in order to open the workbook file. Once you set the password, only someone who knows the password can remove this requirement.
	It's a good idea to save an unprotected copy of your workbook in a secure location before applying password protection. That way, if you forget the password, your data isn't completely lost.
Protect Current Sheet	This is simply another way to access the **Protect Sheet** dialog box.
Protect Workbook Structure	This is simply another way to access the **Protect Structure and Windows** dialog box.
Restrict Access	This option enables you to restrict access to the workbook by using Microsoft's free Information Rights Management (IRM) service. A valid Microsoft account is required to use this feature.
Add a Digital Signature	A signature confirms that the information in the workbook originated from the signer and has not been altered and the signer can be verified (if you possess their certificate).

Note: A full examination of digital signatures and information rights management (IRM) are beyond the scope of this course. For more information on digital signatures or the IRM service, visit **office.microsoft.com**.

Note: For some additional information specific to digital signatures, access the LearnTO **Digitally Sign a Workbook** presentation from the **LearnTO** tile on the CHOICE Course screen.

Metadata

In addition to the sensitive data that may appear within your worksheets, Excel workbook files can contain other sensitive information you may not be aware of. This information includes personal information about the people who worked on the workbook files and sensitive data that may be stored in workbook documents as properties. The general term for this type of information is *metadata*, which literally means "data about other data."

The Document Inspector

Before you share workbooks with colleagues and outside parties, it's a good idea to scan your workbook files for sensitive metadata and to remove that metadata if necessary. You can use Excel's **Document Inspector** to both scan for and determine whether or not to remove such information. The **Document Inspector** scans Excel workbook files for such metadata as comments and other annotations; personal information stored as document properties; hidden rows, columns, and worksheets; and data that is invisible because of formatting applied to cells (such as red text against a red cell background). You can access the **Document Inspector** by selecting **File→Info→Check for Issues→Inspect Document**.

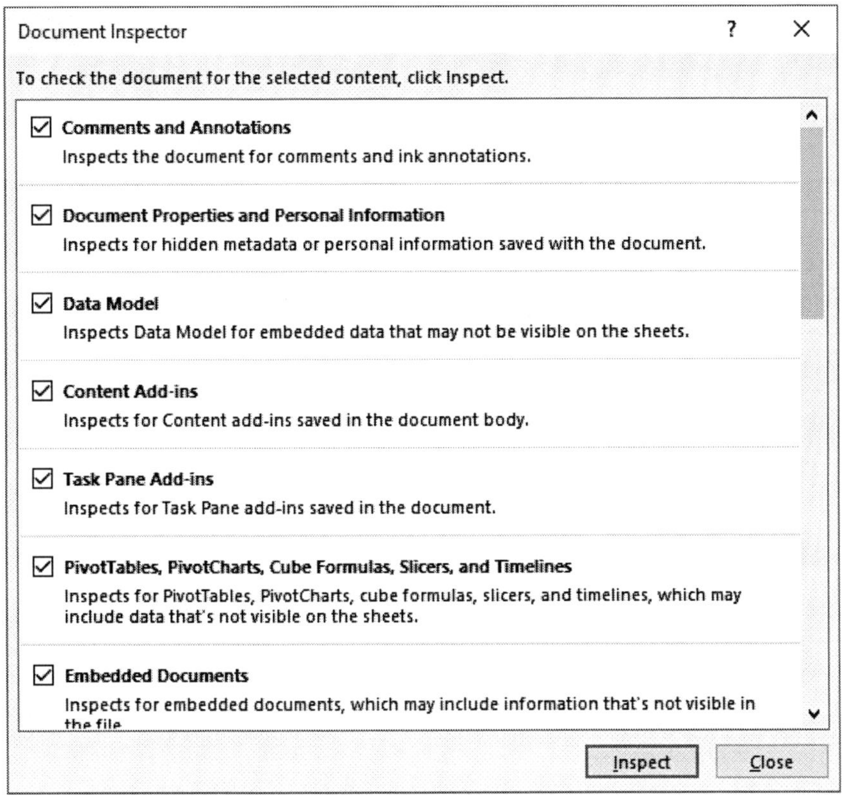

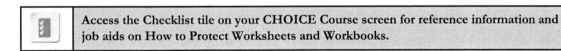

Document Inspector

To check the document for the selected content, click Inspect.

☑ **Comments and Annotations**
Inspects the document for comments and ink annotations.

☑ **Document Properties and Personal Information**
Inspects for hidden metadata or personal information saved with the document.

☑ **Data Model**
Inspects Data Model for embedded data that may not be visible on the sheets.

☑ **Content Add-ins**
Inspects for Content add-ins saved in the document body.

☑ **Task Pane Add-ins**
Inspects for Task Pane add-ins saved in the document.

☑ **PivotTables, PivotCharts, Cube Formulas, Slicers, and Timelines**
Inspects for PivotTables, PivotCharts, cube formulas, slicers, and timelines, which may include data that's not visible on the sheets.

☑ **Embedded Documents**
Inspects for embedded documents, which may include information that's not visible in the file.

Inspect   Close

Figure 3-16: The Document Inspector searches for and enables you to remove potentially sensitive information from your workbooks.

Access the Checklist tile on your **CHOICE** Course screen for reference information and job aids on **How to Protect Worksheets and Workbooks.**

ACTIVITY 3-2
Protecting Worksheets and Workbooks

Before You Begin

The My Regional Salaries.xlsx workbook is open.

Scenario

Your manager is pleased with your work and has asked you to protect the salaries workbook from people seeing the regional worksheets and the formula calculating the average salaries. You decide the best approach for this is to hide the formulas on the Summary worksheet and protect the sheet. You will also need to hide the regional worksheets and protect the structure of the workbook.

1. **Hide the average salary formulas and enable worksheet protection.**
   a) Select the **Summary** worksheet if necessary and select the range **B2:B6**.
   b) Select **Home→Cells→Format→Format Cells**.
   c) In the **Format Cells** dialog box, on the **Protection** tab, select the **Hidden** check box and select **OK**.
   d) Select **Review→Changes→Protect Sheet**.
   e) In the **Protect Sheet** dialog box, in the **Password to unprotect sheet** field type, *sheet* and select **OK**.
   f) In the **Confirm Password** dialog box, in the **Reenter password to proceed** field, type *sheet* and select **OK**.
   g) Verify that you can no longer see the formulas for the range **B2:B6** in the **Formula Bar**.

B2		✕	✓	*fx*	
	A	B	C	D	E
1	Region	Average Salary			
2	Midwest	$67,954			
3	Northeast	$57,354			
4	Southeast	$65,692			
5	Southwest	$67,552			
6	West	$60,402			

   h) Try to change the content in one of the cells on the worksheet.
   i) In the **Microsoft Excel** dialog box indicating that you are trying to change a cell on a protected sheet, select **OK**.
   j) Save the workbook.

2. **Hide the regional worksheets and protect the workbook.**
   a) Select the **Midwest** worksheet and hold the **Shift** key while selecting the **West** worksheet.
   b) Select **Home→Cells→Format→Hide & Unhide→Hide Sheet**.

   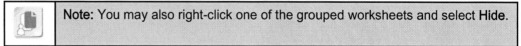

   > **Note:** You may also right-click one of the grouped worksheets and select **Hide**.

c) Verify that all the worksheets except the **Summary** worksheet are hidden.

d) Select **Review→Changes→Protect Workbook**.
e) In the **Protect Structure and Windows** dialog box, in the **Password (optional)** field, type *book* and select **OK**.
f) In the **Confirm Password** dialog box, in the **Reenter password to proceed** field, type *book* and select **OK**.

3. Verify that users cannot see the hidden worksheets.

a) Select **Home→Cells→Format**.
b) Observe how the commands to manage the structure of the workbook are disabled.

4. Add a password to open the workbook.

a) Select **File→Info→Protect Workbook→Encrypt with Password**.
b) In the **Encrypt Document** dialog box, in the **Password** field, type *password* and select **OK**.

c) In the **Confirm Password** dialog box, in the **Reenter password** field, type *password* and select **OK**.

d) Verify that the **Protect Workbook** section updates indicating that a password is required to open the workbook.

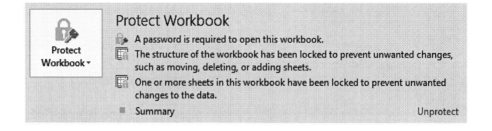

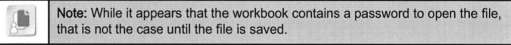

Note: While it appears that the workbook contains a password to open the file, that is not the case until the file is saved.

e) Save the workbook and close the file.

5. **Verify that the passwords you have entered protect the file from unwanted access.**

a) In Excel, open the **My Regional Salaries.xlsx** workbook.
b) In the **Password** dialog box, in the **Password** field, type *password* and select **OK**.
c) Verify that the file opens with the worksheet and workbook protected.
d) Close the file.

Summary

In this lesson, you collaborated on workbooks and applied security measures to maintain the integrity of your data. The ability to work with colleagues and clients on a variety of projects is a must in today's ever-connected environment. But this level of collaboration brings with it the risk of lost, stolen, or corrupted data. Your ability to balance collaboration and security considerations means you can get the input and the feedback you need without having to worry about your sensitive information.

In your current role, do you see using change tracking or merging content from shared workbooks as the best option for collaboration?

Do you feel more comfortable including sensitive information in workbooks that you need to share with other users now that you're aware of Excel's protection capabilities? Why?

Note: Check your CHOICE Course screen for opportunities to interact with your classmates, peers, and the larger CHOICE online community about the topics covered in this course or other topics you are interested in. From the Course screen you can also access available resources for a more continuous learning experience.

4 Automating Workbook Functionality

Lesson Time: 1 hour

Lesson Introduction

Working with large workbooks presents a number of challenges. Entering large amounts of data can be time consuming and prone to errors. You may also find yourself spending a lot of time and effort performing the same few tasks over and over again. And, the more people who work in the same workbook, the more these types of issues become magnified. In short, as you develop ever larger and more complex workbooks, you'll want to find ways to automate any number of tasks to save time, reduce errors, and generally make using your workbooks easier.

The good news is that Microsoft® Office Excel® 2016 includes a variety of features that enable you to do just that. From ensuring that only the correct data or type of data can be entered into your worksheets, to performing repetitive tasks so you don't have to, Excel's automation features can save you valuable time and keep your data intact.

Lesson Objectives

In this lesson, you will automate workbook functionality. You will:

- Apply data validation.

- Search for invalid data and formulas with errors.

- Work with macros.

TOPIC A

Apply Data Validation

The single most important aspect of data analysis is having accurate data to analyze. Given the large number of people who may use your workbooks, it's essential that you be able to trust the data they enter. Even just a few bad entries can have a chain-reaction-like effect on formulas and tables throughout large workbooks. But, what can you do, short of standing over someone's shoulder as he or she enters data, to ensure your data is accurate? This seems a near-impossible task to achieve.

Fortunately, Excel provides you with a robust and flexible way to help ensure only valid data is entered into your worksheets: data validation. Understanding precisely what Excel enables you to control, and how to configure your worksheets to accept only correct entries, will let you to take control of your worksheets and be assured that you're avoiding major data errors that could take hours to locate and resolve.

Data Validation

In Excel, you use *data validation* to restrict data entries in worksheet cells. You can use data validation, for example, to limit cell entries to values above, below, or between particular thresholds; to only positive values; to only date values; or even to one of a selection of options from a drop-down menu. Data validation helps ensure that your worksheet users cannot enter data that would cause unwanted results by enabling you to define restrictions on the data they enter. Data that does not meet the requirements of data validation is known as invalid data.

It is important to keep a few things in mind when applying data validation to your workbooks. First, data validation does not work on data that is copied and pasted or dragged to a cell; it works only on data that is manually entered. In fact, copying data to a cell where you have applied data validation may clear the data validation from the cell. Additionally, although you can apply data validation to cells that already contain data, Excel will not notify you about, nor change any, existing data that does not meet the specified data validation criteria. Data validation is best suited for preventing erroneous data entries, not malicious attempts to corrupt data. Use cell protection, instead, to prevent users from purposefully entering bad data.

The Data Validation Dialog Box

You will use the **Data Validation** dialog box to apply data validation to worksheet cells and to manage existing data validation criteria. The **Data Validation** dialog box is divided into three tabs, the **Settings**, **Input Message**, and **Error Alert** tabs, which provide you with access to the commands and functions you will use to create and manage data validation and data validation messages. You can access the **Data Validation** dialog box by selecting **Data→Data Tools→Data Validation**.

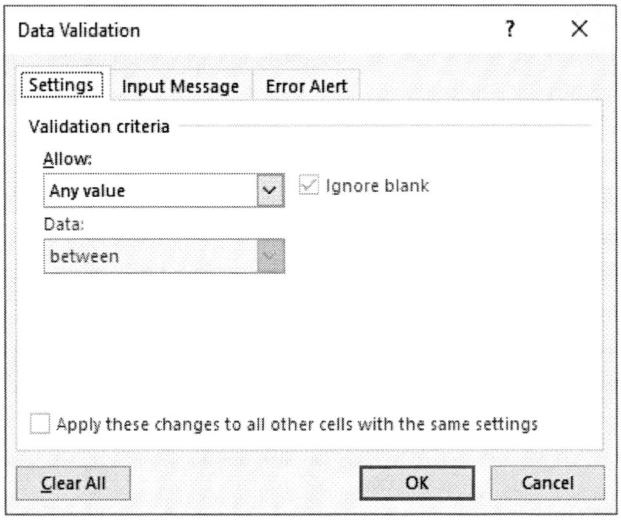

Figure 4–1: Use the Data Validation dialog box to apply and manage data validation criteria.

Data Validation Criteria

Excel provides you with a variety of criteria you can use to control what users can enter into worksheet cells. By default, you can enter any value into any cell on a worksheet. Excel provides you with seven other types of data validation criteria that you can apply to worksheet cells, which you can access from the **Allow** drop-down menu on the **Settings** tab of the **Data Validation** dialog box. You can also customize your data validation criteria by using a formula. The particular options available on the **Settings** tab change depending on the type of criteria you select from the **Allow** drop-down menu.

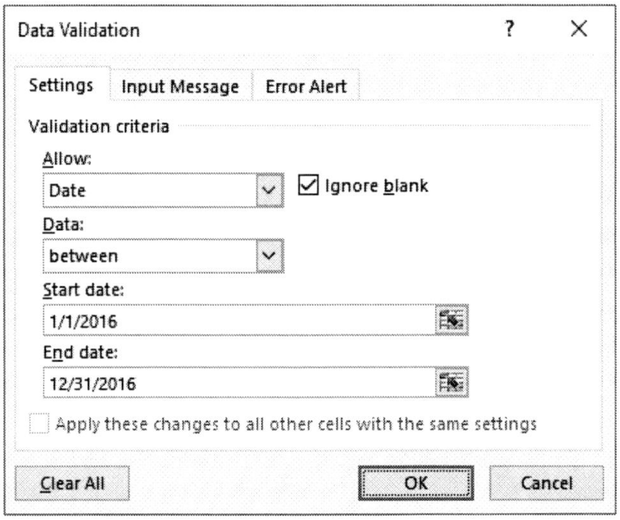

Figure 4–2: Excel provides various options for configuring data validation based on the selected criteria type.

The following table describes the various categories of data validation criteria.

Data Validation Criteria Type	Description
Any value	This is the default setting for worksheet cells. It enables users to enter any type of data in cells.

Data Validation Criteria Type	Description
Whole number	This criteria type allows users to enter only whole numbers that meet the specified conditions, which are based on comparison operators. So, for example, you can allow users to enter only whole numbers greater than 50, between 13 and 57, or less than or equal to 1,000.
Decimal	This criteria type is nearly identical to the whole number criteria type. The only exception is that it allows for values containing decimals.
List	This criteria type enables you to set a predetermined list of options as the only valid entries for the cells. You can either enter the list of options directly into the **Data Validation** dialog box, or you can reference a range of cells that contain the valid entries. This criteria type enables you to provide users with in-cell drop-down menus they can use to enter the data. You can also opt to allow them to manually enter the list items.
Date	This criteria type is similar to both the whole number and the decimal criteria types, but it allows users to enter only date values.
Time	This is the same as the date criteria type with the exception that it restricts data entries to time values.
Text length	This criteria type allows users to enter only values that contain a specified number of characters. The text criteria type does not limit values to only text values, you can also enter numeric or other values as long as they contain the specified number of characters.
Custom	This criteria type enables you to customize your data validation by using formulas to limit data entries.

Whereas the options that Excel displays in the **Data Validation** dialog box change depending on the criteria type selected, there are two options that always appear. The first of these is the **Ignore blank** check box. Although this check box is always available, it pertains only to criteria that are based on references to a data range; this is common when creating a list, for example. If the **Ignore blank** check box is checked and the source criteria (range) contains blank cells, then users are able to enter any value into the cells with the data validation applied to them. If the **Ignore blank** check box is not checked, users will receive whatever error you specified for the data validation if they try to enter a value not contained in the source criteria.

The other option that is always present, although it is grayed out until you have actually applied data validation criteria to the selected cell(s), is the **Apply these changes to all other cells with the same settings** check box. This check box pertains only to editing data validation. If you have a range of cells to which you've applied the same data validation and you select only one of those cells for the purpose of editing the data validation criteria, this check box determines whether or not the changes will affect all of the other cells with the same data validation applied to them.

Input Messages

In addition to specifying which types of data users can enter into worksheet cells, Excel provides you with options for prompting users with messages and warnings regarding data validation. You will use the commands and options on the **Input Message** and **Error Alert** tabs in the **Data Validation** dialog box to create and manage these messages. Input messages serve to provide the user with instructional text on what type of data can be entered into the cell. Setting input messages does not restrict the user from being able to enter invalid data; they simply display whatever message you specify. Input messages appear in a pop-up window that opens when users select cells containing data validation that has input messages enabled.

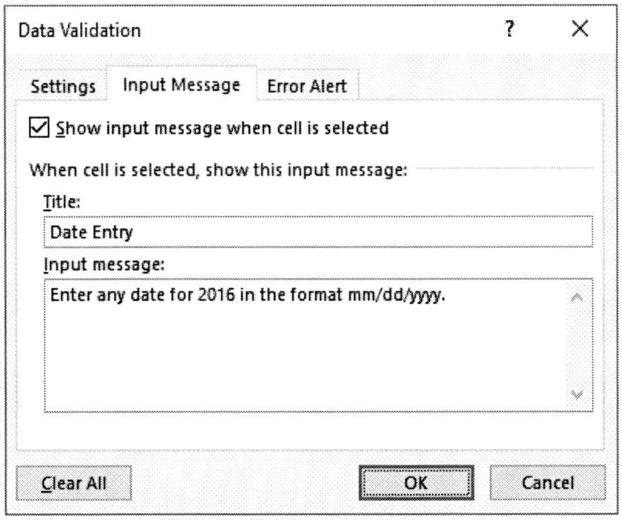

Figure 4-3: Input messages do not restrict the entry of data; they simply prompt the user to enter particular data.

The following table describes the functions of the various elements of the **Input Message** tab in the **Data Validation** dialog box.

Input Message Tab Element	Description
Show input message when cell is selected check box	Activates or deactivates input messages for the selected cell or range.
Title field	Enables you to enter a title for the input message. The title will appear at the top of the input message pop-up window when users select the cells with data validation applied to them.
Input message field	Enables you to enter the input message that will appear in the input message pop-up window.

Error Alerts

Error alerts can either simply warn users they have entered invalid data or they can restrict the entry of invalid data. Excel displays error alerts in a dialog box when users enter invalid data into cells that contain data validation. There are three styles of error alert you can define for cells that contain data validation: **Information**, **Warning**, or **Stop**.

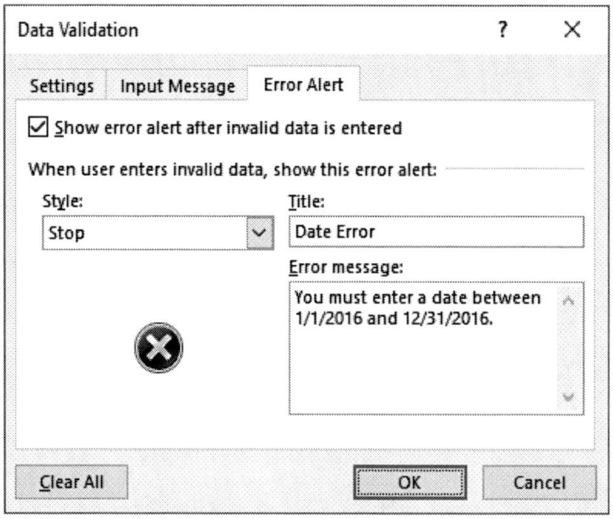

Figure 4-4: Excel displays warning messages in a dialog box. Depending on the error message level you set, Excel will either warn users about entering invalid data or it will restrict them from entering it.

The following table describes the functions of the various elements of the **Error Alert** tab in the **Data Validation** dialog box.

Error Alert Tab Element	Description
Show error alert after invalid data is entered check box	Activates or deactivates error alerts for the selected cell or range. As the error alert style determines whether or not Excel restricts the entry of invalid data, this essentially toggles the data validation itself on or off.
Style drop-down menu	Enables you to select the desired error alert style.
Title field	Enables you to enter a title for the error alert. The title you enter here becomes the name of the dialog box that displays the error alert message.
Error message field	Enables you to enter an error alert message.

The following table describes the three error alert styles and their meaning.

Error Alert Style	Description
Stop	The **Stop** error alert restricts users from entering any invalid data. When Excel displays **Stop** error alerts, the user has only two options: to cancel or to retry the entry.
Warning	The **Warning** error alert will allow users to enter invalid data, but it first prompts them to decide whether or not they wish to continue.
Information	The **Information** error alert is the least restrictive of the three. Although it does display the specified error alert message, users can simply select **OK** to continue entering the invalid data.

Access the Checklist tile on your CHOICE Course screen for reference information and job aids on How to Apply Data Validation Criteria.

ACTIVITY 4-1
Applying Data Validation

Data File

C:\091057Data\Automating Workbook Functionality\Regional Expenses.xlsx

Before You Begin

Excel 2016 is open.

Scenario

As finance manager for Develetech Industries you have been compiling the expenses for each of the regions in the business. You want to ensure the data you enter in the workbook are within the correct parameters. You decide to add data validation to several cells and ranges to prevent data entry errors.

1. Open the **Regional Expenses.xlsx** workbook.
   a) Navigate to the **C:\091057Data\Automating Workbook Functionality** folder and open the **Regional Expenses.xlsx** workbook.
   b) Save the file as *My Regional Expenses.xlsx*.

2. Enable and configure the settings for data validation for expense reporter.
   a) Verify that the **North American** worksheet is selected and select cell **B3**.
   b) Select **Data→Data Tools→Data Validation**.
   c) In the **Data Validation** dialog box, select the **Settings** tab if necessary, and in the **Allow** drop-down list, select **List**.
   d) Select the **Source** field, then select **Formulas→Defined Names→Use in Formula** and select **Reported_By**.
   e) Verify that the **Source** field is **=Reported_By**.

3. Configure the input message for data validation.

    a) In the **Data Validation** dialog box, select the **Input Message** tab.
    b) Verify that **Show input message when cell is selected** check box is selected.
    c) Select the **Title** field and type *Expense Reporter*
    d) Press **Tab** and in the **Input message** field, type *Select the person reporting the expense.*
    e) Verify the **Input Message** settings.

4. Configure the error alert for data validation.

    a) In the **Data Validation** dialog box, select the **Error Alert** tab.
    b) Verify that **Show error alert after invalid data is entered** check box is selected.
    c) Verify that the **Style** drop-down list has **Stop** selected.
    d) Select the **Title** field and type *Reported By Error*
    e) Select the **Error message** field and type *Please select a user from the list.*
    f) Verify the **Error Alert** settings and select **OK**.

g) Verify that cell **B3** is selected and that the **Input Message** is displayed.

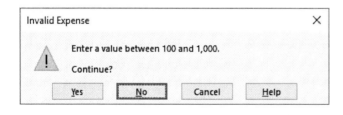

h) Enter your first name in cell **B3**.
i) In the **Reported By Error** dialog box, select **Cancel**.

5. Apply data validation to the expense values.

a) Select the range **B6:E9**.
b) Select **Data→Data Tools→Data Validation**.
c) In the **Data Validation** dialog box, select the **Settings** tab if necessary, and in the **Allow** drop-down list, select **Decimal**.
d) Verify that in the **Data** drop-down list **between** is selected.
e) Select the **Minimum** field and type *100*
f) Select the **Maximum** field and type *1,000*
g) Select the **Input Message** tab and uncheck the **Show input message when cell is selected** check box.
h) Select the **Error Alert** tab, then select the **Style** drop-down arrow and select **Warning**.
i) Select the **Title** field and type *Invalid Expense*
j) Select the **Error message** field and type *Enter a value between 100 and 1,000.*
k) Select **OK**.

6. Test data validation

a) Select cell **B3** and select the drop-down arrow that appears to the right of the cell.
b) Select **Claire Gibbs**.
c) Select cell **E6** and enter *10,000*
d) Verify that the error alert **Invalid Expense** appears.

Invalid Expense	✕
⚠ Enter a value between 100 and 1,000.	
Continue?	
Yes	No	Cancel	Help

 Note: An Error Alert with a Style set to Warning will allow for non-standard or aberrant data entry.

e) Select **Yes**.
f) In cell **E7** enter *525.75*

7. Save the workbook and keep the file open.

TOPIC B

Search for Invalid Data and Formulas with Errors

Although it's handy to be able to trace a cell to its precedent and dependent cells, you won't always immediately be able to recognize where an error exists within your worksheets. In these cases, you'll need a way to scan entire worksheets to locate particular types of errors out of all of the data, formulas, and functions they contain. Fortunately, Excel provides you with access to two useful features for doing so: error checking and invalid data markup. Taking advantage of these features means you won't have to know ahead of time which cells contain errors, and you'll be able to scan even the largest worksheets for errors in just a few moments.

Invalid Data

In Excel, *invalid data* is any cell data that does not meet the criteria specified in data validation applied to the cell. Cells that you have not applied data validation criteria to cannot contain invalid data.

The Circle Invalid Data Command

You will use the **Circle Invalid Data** command to quickly identify cells on a worksheet that contain invalid data. When you execute this command, Excel scans the currently selected worksheet for invalid data and temporarily displays a red circle or oval around any cells containing invalid data. These circles disappear after a short period of time and whenever you save the workbook, so you may have to re-display them if it takes some length of time to identify and correct all instances of invalid data. You can access this command by selecting **Data→Data Tools→Data Validation drop-down arrow→Circle Invalid Data**.

◢	A	B	C	D	E
1	**Develetech Industries - Expenses**				
2					
3	**Entered By**	Jerald			
4					
5	**Expense**	**Quarter 1**	**Quarter 2**	**Quarter 3**	**Quarter 4**
6	**Fixed expenses**	10000	175	459	207
7	**Flexible expenses**	172	247	113	207
8	**Discretionary expenses**	158	244	180	428
9	**Miscellaneous**	319	103	275	286
10	**Total**	$10,649	$769	$1,027	$1,128
11					
12	**Date Completed**	12/31/2015			
13					

Figure 4-5: Circled instances of invalid data on an Excel worksheet.

The Error Checking Command

You are already familiar with the kinds of errors that can occur within Excel worksheets. The relatively minor errors, such as an inconsistent formula, that may return a valid value from a function but Excel still flags as something you want to check, and major errors, such as the #DIV/0! error, that do not return a valid value from a function. Excel flags the former with a small green triangle in the corner of the cell, whereas the latter returns an error value in the cells themselves. On smaller worksheets, these errors are relatively easy to spot. But on very large worksheets, you might have to scroll through thousands of rows and columns of data to locate them. Fortunately, Excel provides you with a single command that enables you to scan entire worksheets to locate and identify all of the errors they contain with ease: the **Error Checking** command.

If Excel finds errors on a worksheet, it displays the **Error Checking** dialog box. From here you can browse through all errors on the worksheet, search for Help resources about the errors, and manage how you would like to resolve the errors. You can check a worksheet for errors by selecting **Formulas→Formula Auditing→Error Checking**.

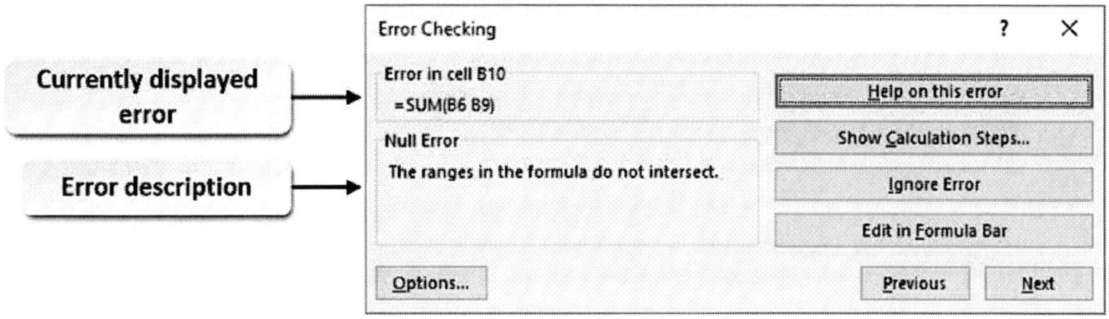

Figure 4-6: The Error Checking dialog box.

The following table describes the various elements of the **Error Checking** dialog box.

Error Checking Dialog Box Element	Description
Currently displayed error	Identifies the location and displays the contents of the currently displayed error.
Error description	Displays a description of the currently displayed error.
Options button	Opens the **Excel Options** dialog box with the **Formulas** tab selected. From there, you can configure Excel's error checking options.
Help on this error button	Opens the **Excel Help** window with search results for Help resources about the currently displayed error. If you have Excel Help set to only search for Help resources on your computer, this command simply opens the **Excel Help** window; no resources are automatically displayed.
Copy Formula from Above button	If the error is due to an inconsistent formula or function, selecting this button will copy the formula or function from the cell above the cell containing the currently displayed error to the cell containing the error.
Show Calculation Steps button	Opens the **Evaluate Formula** dialog box, which you can use to determine what part of a formula or function is causing an error.
Ignore Error button	Leaves the cell content associated with the currently displayed error as it is.
Edit in Formula Bar button	Opens the formula or function causing the currently displayed error in the **Formula Bar** for editing.
Previous button	Displays the previous worksheet error in the **Error Checking** dialog box.
Next button	Displays the next worksheet error in the **Error Checking** dialog box.

Note: The longer command buttons to the right of the **Error Checking** dialog box can change depending on the currently displayed error. This table describes the most commonly encountered of these.

Error Types

It is one thing to be able to locate and identify which cells contain errors; it is something else entirely to know how to resolve errors once you've identified them. There are seven major types of errors that will return an error value in worksheet cells instead of flagging the issue with a green error icon. The following table identifies and describes these seven error values and identifies common solutions to them.

Error Value	Excel Returns This Error When	Resolution(s)
#NULL!	You use an intersection operator (which is a blank space between range references) with two ranges that don't actually intersect.	Either replace the intersection operator with the intended operator or correct the range references to two ranges that intersect.
#DIV/0!	A formula or a function is trying to divide some value by zero. This can also be caused when a formula or function is trying to divide by the value in a blank cell.	Replace the value zero with the correct numeric value, correct the cell reference to a populated cell, or correct the formula or function that is returning the zero that Excel is trying to divide by.
#VALUE!	When a formula or function is referencing an incorrect data type. For example, if a function is asking Excel to multiply a numerical value by a text label.	Correct the data entry causing the error to the correct data type, or correct a formula or function so that it returns the correct data type.
#REF!	A formula or a function contains an invalid reference. This typically occurs when you delete a row or column (not just the values in the cells) containing cells a formula or function is referencing.	Restore the deleted cells or update the references in the formula or function.
#NAME?	It does not recognize text that you include in a formula or function. Common causes of this are misspelling a defined name, misspelling the name of a function or a nested function, excluding quotation marks around text that requires them, and omitting the range operator (:) in a range in a function.	Correct the spelling of the defined name or function, use the **Paste Name** dialog box or the Formula AutoComplete feature instead of typing defined names, add quotation marks around text in function arguments, or add the range operator to range references that are missing one.
#NUM!	An argument in a function that should be a numeric value is some other data type. This error can also be caused by a calculation that returns a numeric value that is too small or too large for Excel to express.	Revise the function or the data feeding the function to ensure that all arguments are of the correct data type, or revise the formula or function to return a numeric value that Excel can express.

Error Value	Excel Returns This Error When	Resolution(s)
#N/A	A function or a formula cannot access a required value. Common causes of this error include an invalid **lookup_value** argument in Lookup functions, trying to use Lookup functions to search an unsorted dataset, using array functions with different sized arrays, and omitting required arguments from functions.	Ensure that the **lookup_value** argument in a Lookup function is valid, sort the dataset you are searching with a Lookup function, ensure that all arrays in array formulas are the same size, and ensure that all functions include all required arguments.

Access the Checklist tile on your CHOICE Course screen for reference information and job aids on **How to Search for Invalid Data and Formulas with Errors.**

ACTIVITY 4-2
Searching for Invalid Data and Formulas with Errors

Before You Begin
The workbook **My Regional Expenses.xlsx** is open.

Scenario
Continuing in your role as finance manager for Develetech Industries, you have done your best to verify that the data entered for each region is correct. You now want to check for invalid data and any problems with formulas. You decide to circle invalid data and fix inaccurate entries.

1. **Find invalid data entries on the Europe worksheet.**
   a) Select the **European** worksheet.
   b) Select **Data→Data Tools→Data Validation drop-down arrow→Circle Invalid Data**.
   c) Verify that there are two cells that contain invalid data.

	A	B
1	Develetech Industries - European Expenses	
2		
3	Reported By	Jerald
4		
5	Expense	Quarter 1
6	Fixed expenses	10000

2. **Fix invalid data on the worksheet.**
   a) Select cell **B6** and enter *280*

    Note: After you enter the correct value, the invalid data circle should disappear. If not, you will clear validation circles later in this activity.

   b) Select cell **B3** and select the drop-down arrow that appears to the right of the cell.

    Note: The Input Message and Error Alert data validation settings on the European worksheet are not the same as the data validation settings on the North American worksheet.

   c) Select **Jerald Maldonado**.
   d) Select **Data→Data Tools→Data Validation drop-down arrow→Clear Validation Circles**.

3. **Check the worksheet for errors in formulas.**
   a) Navigate to cell **A1**.
   b) Select **Formulas→Formula Auditing→Error Checking**.

c) Verify that the **Error Checking** dialog box found an error in cell **B10**.

Error Checking	? ✕
Error in cell B10 =SUM(B6 B9)	Help on this error
	Show Calculation Steps...
Null Error The ranges in the formula do not intersect.	Ignore Error
	Edit in Formula Bar
Options...	Previous Next

d) Select **Edit in Formula Bar**.

e) Correct the error by typing a *colon (:)* between the range **B6:B9**. The formula should be **=SUM(B6:B9)**.

f) Press **Enter**.

g) In the **Error Checking** dialog box select **Resume**.

h) In the **Microsoft Excel** dialog box, verify that the error check is complete and select **OK**.

Microsoft Excel	✕
⚠ The error check is complete for the entire sheet.	
OK	

4. Save the workbook and keep the file open.

TOPIC C

Work with Macros

If you've developed Excel workbooks for any length of time, especially if you create numerous workbooks for similar purposes, you've likely found yourself performing the same mundane tasks over and over again. Perhaps you create new financial reports every quarter or period. If so, the labels, formatting, formulas and functions, and overall layout are likely the same each time. Or, perhaps you're a project manager who uses Excel to track major milestones. The workbook for each new project likely contains a lot of the same information. Whatever the reason, performing the same tasks over and over just feels like a waste of time.

If you find yourself feeling frustrated over performing the same repetitive, non-value-added tasks each time you create a workbook, you're in luck. Excel 2016 supports a powerful feature that can actually perform these tasks for you: macros. By unlocking the nearly endless capabilities macros can offer, you will not only save yourself time and effort, but you'll also begin to open up whole new worlds of automation you may have never even realized were possible.

Macros

A *macro*, in its simplest terms, is a series of steps or instructions that you can run from a single command or action. In Excel, as with some other Office applications, you can either record macros or write them in Microsoft® Visual Basic® for Application (VBA) code using the Visual Basic Editor. You can use macros any time you would like Excel to perform a repetitive series of steps, such as filling in commonly used labels, formatting data and graphics to suit a particular purpose or to adhere to organizational branding requirements, or entering formulas and functions that you use in multiple workbooks. There are several options you can use to run macros once you've created them. These include running them from a dialog box, assigning keyboard shortcuts, and using controls. You can even create macros that run automatically when you open a workbook.

You can work with macros only in Excel workbooks that have been saved as macro-enabled workbooks. The file extension for these workbooks is .xlsm. Keep in mind that macros can be associated with security risks as they require you to run code within your workbooks. Always check with your system administrator for your organization's security requirements for working with macros.

Macro Security Settings

Although you know you can trust your own macros, that may not be the case with macros created by someone else. Macros may be convenient, but there's always a chance you will introduce malicious code to your system or network by running macros from outside sources. Excel 2016 provides you with a number of options you can select from in terms of macro security settings. The easiest way to access these settings is by selecting **Developer→Code→Macro Security**. You can also access them by selecting **Trust Center Settings** on the **Trust Center** tab in the **Excel Options** dialog box, and then selecting the **Macro Settings** tab in the **Trust Center** dialog box.

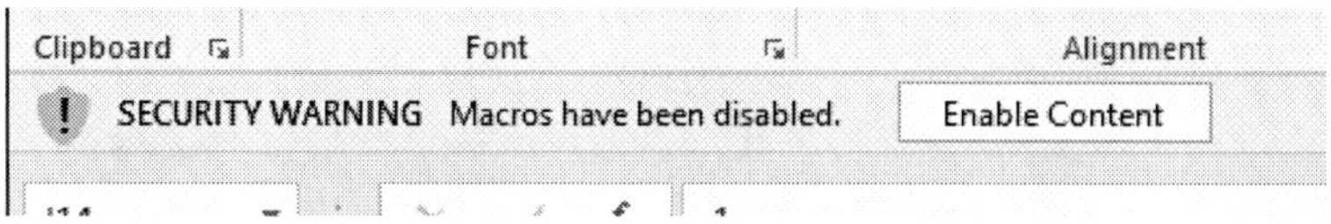

Figure 4–7: Depending on your macro security settings, workbooks containing macros may display a warning message when you open them.

Note: The **Developer** tab is often hidden from the ribbon and can be shown by selecting **File**→**Options**→**Customize Ribbon** and selecting the **Developer** check box.

The following table describes the various macro security settings, as well as the additional security option for developers in the **Trust Center**.

Macro Security Option	Description
Disable all macros without notification	This is the strongest security setting. Selecting this option disables all macros and any warnings Excel would otherwise display regarding macros. You can, however, establish a trusted folder, save macro-enabled workbooks in it, and still run the macros with this option selected.
Disable all macros with notification	This option enables you to decide whether or not to run macros upon opening macro-enabled workbooks. Excel will display a warning and prompt you to decide whether or not to enable macros. This is the default setting in Excel 2016.
Disable all macros except digitally signed macros	This setting is similar to the **Disable all macros with notification** option. The only difference here is that Excel automatically enables macros in workbooks from publishers you have trusted without displaying a message. If you open macro-enabled workbooks from non-trusted publishers, Excel will prompt you to decide.
Enable all macros	This is the least-secure option, which is typically not recommended. If you select this option, Excel will enable and allow you to run any macro in any macro-enabled workbook.
Trust access to the VBA project object model check box	This is a separate option from the macro security settings that should be used only by developers who have extensive knowledge of the Visual Basic coding environment. Basically, this option either blocks or allows code to access Office applications at the code level for purposes of automating Office functionality.

Microsoft Visual Basic for Applications

As previously mentioned, you can either record macros or use *Visual Basic for Applications* code to write them. Visual Basic for Applications is the programming language developers use for Microsoft Office applications and other related add-ins, macros, and applications. When you record a macro in Excel, your actions are recorded as VBA code; the coding work is done for you. The advantage to coding your macros manually in VBA instead of recording them is that you have a far greater level of control over what the macro does. Many users don't have extensive knowledge of VBA, so they prefer to record their macros. Some experienced users often prefer to start by recording a macro and then edit the code to make small adjustments to it.

You write and edit VBA code by using Microsoft's *Visual Basic Editor*, which is included with Excel 2016. The VB Editor is made up of several major components that you can use to navigate, inspect, and edit your macros. Saved macros are stored in folders called *modules*, which you can view in the VB Editor. Modules are saved along with the workbook file of the workbook in which you saved the macro, and they appear as part of the workbook's hierarchical structure in the VB Editor user interface.

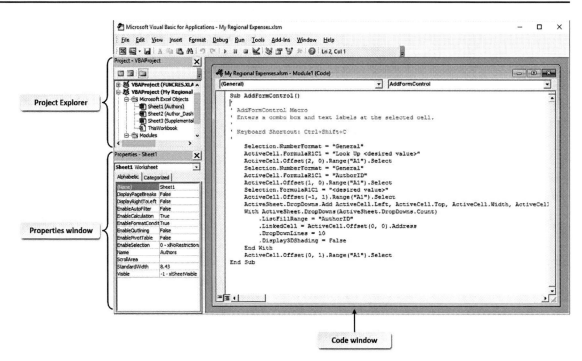

Figure 4-8: Use the Visual Basic Editor to write and edit your macro code.

The following table describes the main components of the Visual Basic Editor user interface.

Visual Basic Editor Component	Description
Project Explorer	Displays the hierarchical structure of objects in all open workbooks. This includes the worksheets in each workbook, any VBA modules, and VBA UserForms.
Properties window	Displays the properties of the object selected in the **Project Explorer**. The VB Editor does not display the **Properties** window by default. You can open it from the **View** menu in the VB Editor menu bar.
Code window	Displays VBA code. It is in the **Code** window that you can write and edit macro code.

The Record Macro Dialog Box

You will use the **Record Macro** dialog box to begin the process of recording macros. From here, you can name the macro and select a location to save it. Optionally, you can also assign a keyboard shortcut that will run the macro. And, you have the option of adding a description to the macro to inform users of what, precisely, the macro does. You can access the **Record Macro** dialog box by selecting **View→Macros→Macros drop-down arrow→Record Macro** or from **Developer→Code→Record Macro**.

 Note: While it is not possible to customize keyboard shortcuts in Excel 2016, as you can assign them to macros, you can use macros as a workaround to create keyboard shortcuts.

Once you begin recording a macro, nearly every action you perform in Excel becomes part of the macro code's instructions, including errors. So, it is sometimes necessary, especially for users who are new to macros, to delete a macro and record it over again. With time and a little experience, you'll begin to get a feel for how your macros will run based on the actions you record.

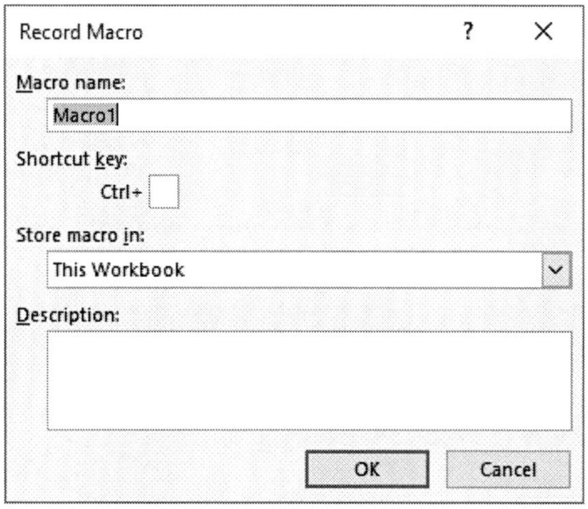

Figure 4-9: Use the Record Macro dialog box to begin the process of recording a macro.

The Use Relative References Command

When you record macros, you can record nearly any action that accomplishes a task in Excel, such as selecting a cell, a range, or a command; or entering data in a cell. As such, you can record the process of adding data and formulas to cells. This means absolute and relative cell references become extremely important. Just as a simple example, let's say you record the process of entering the following data and formula into an Excel worksheet.

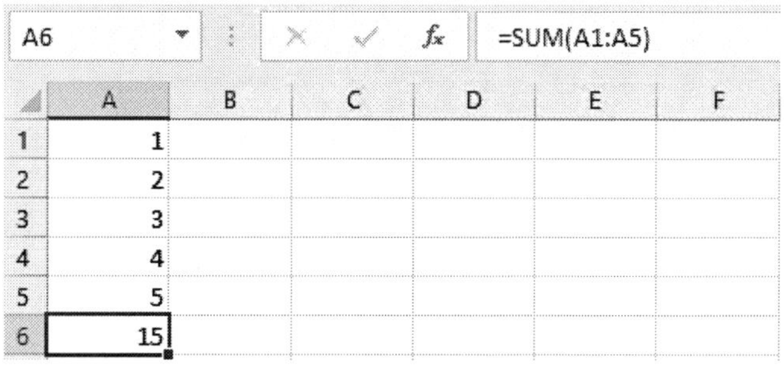

Figure 4-10: Excel worksheet example.

If you use absolute references when you record the macro, when you run the macro, it will always enter the values and the formula in the range **A1:A6**. If you use relative references, it will place the values and the formula in six consecutive cells within the same column starting at the currently selected cell.

To control whether Excel records the macro by using relative or absolute references, toggle the **Use Relative References** command on or off. You can even toggle it on and off during the same recording so you can use a mix of absolute and relative references within the same macro. You can access the **Use Relative References** command by selecting **View→Macros→Macros drop-down arrow→Use Relative References** or by selecting **Developer→Code→Use Relative References**.

The Macro Dialog Box

You will use the **Macro** dialog box to manage and run your macros. In the **Macro** dialog box, you can view all available macros, run them, delete them, open them in the Visual Basic Editor to edit or debug them, and configure keyboard shortcuts. You can access the **Macro** dialog box by selecting **View→Macros→Macros drop-down arrow→View Macros** or **Developer→Code→Macros**.

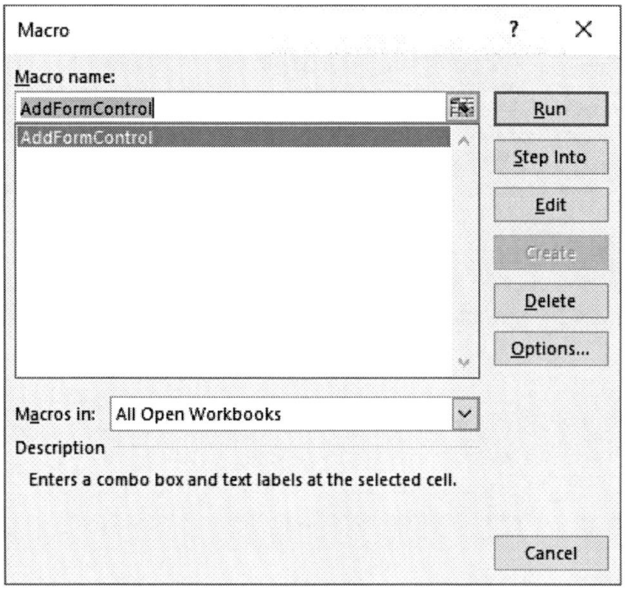

Figure 4-11: Use the Macro dialog box to manage your macros.

Note: If you have more than one workbook open when you open the **Macro** dialog box, macro names for any workbook that isn't the currently selected workbook will appear with the workbook file name followed by an exclamation point (!) before the macro name.

The following table describes the functions of the various elements of the **Macro** dialog box.

Macro Dialog Box Element	Function
Run button	Executes the currently selected macro.
Step Into button	Opens the selected macro's code in the VB Editor for the purpose of debugging the code. Once the macro is open in the VB Editor, you can press the **F8** key to step through the macro one instruction at a time. This way, you can watch the macro run on the worksheet and view the code associated with the action simultaneously. At each step, the VB Editor highlights the corresponding code.
Edit button	Opens the selected macro's code in the VB Editor so you can edit it.
Create button	Normally, this button is inactive. However, if a macro name is typed into the **Macro name** field, the **Create** button is active.
Delete button	Deletes the selected macro.
Options button	Opens the **Macro Options** dialog box. From here, you can assign or change the macro's keyboard shortcut, or add or edit its description.
Macros in drop-down menu	Selects which macros Excel displays in the **Macro** dialog box.

Macro Names

All macros must have a name. And, as with other named items in Excel, you must follow a particular convention when naming your macros. Macro names:

- Must begin with a letter.
- Must contain only letters, numbers, and underscores (_).
- Cannot contain any spaces.
- Should not be the same as cell references, as this may result in errors.

If you name a macro *Auto_Open*, Excel will automatically run the macro when you open the workbook that contains it.

The Personal Workbook

Although you can save macros in individual workbooks, when you do, you can use the macros only in the workbooks they're saved in. But you may also wish to create macros for use in other workbooks. In such cases, you can save the macro in a hidden workbook called the *personal workbook*. The first time you save a macro to your personal workbook, Excel automatically creates the workbook and names it PERSONAL.XLSB. This workbook automatically opens every time you open Excel on your computer once Excel creates it, which is why you can use macros saved here in any other macro-enabled workbook on your computer.

As the personal workbook is a hidden workbook, you will not be able to see it when you open Excel. If you wish to edit or delete a macro that you have saved to your personal workbook, you must first unhide the PERSONAL.XLSB workbook and then edit or delete the macro. You can then re-hide your personal workbook if you don't wish to view it every time you open Excel. After saving a new macro to the personal workbook, Excel will prompt you to save the personal workbook the next time you close Excel. You must save the personal workbook for the new macro to be available in other workbooks.

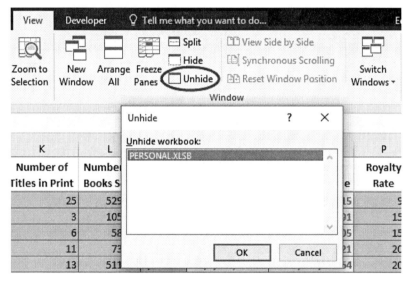

Figure 4–12: You must unhide the personal workbook to delete or edit macros that are saved there.

Copying Macros

In addition to storing macros in the personal workbook, you can copy and paste a macro that you'd like to use in another workbook directly to the other workbook using the VB Editor. This enables you to reuse macro code in other workbooks without having to make it available by saving the macro code to the personal workbook. As with recording macros, you'll need to save the workbook you wish to copy the macro code to as a macro-enabled workbook. If the destination workbook does not already contain macros, you'll also need to add a module to it in order to create the **Modules** folder for the workbook. Often, it's a best practice to create a new module for the copied macro code anyway, but you can add new code to an existing macro.

 Access the Checklist tile on your CHOICE Course screen for reference information and job aids on How to Work with Macros.

ACTIVITY 4-3
Creating a Macro

Before You Begin
The workbook **My Regional Expenses.xlsx** is open.

Scenario
Your workbook is taking shape and you realize that you have yet to add formatting on all the worksheets. Since the three regional worksheets have the same structure, you want to apply the same formatting to each of them.

You want to make the following formatting changes to the North American, European, and Australian worksheets:

- Change the formatting of each of the worksheet titles in cell A1 to bold, italic, and 14 pts.
- Bold, italicize, and underline the expense headings in column A, as well as the quarter headings in row 5.
- Format the values and totals for each quarter with currency formatting.

  Rather than format each of the worksheets manually, you decide to format the North American worksheet while recording a macro. You will then automate the formatting of the other worksheets.

---

1. Begin recording the macro to format the worksheets.
   a) Select the **North American** worksheet.
   b) Select **View→Macros→Macros drop-down arrow→Record Macro**.
   c) In the **Record Macro** dialog box, in the **Macro name** field, type *FormatSheet* and press **Tab**.
   d) Observe that the cursor is in the **Shortcut key** field and that **Ctrl+** is preconfigured, press **Shift+F** to produce the shortcut key, **Ctrl+Shift+F**.
   e) In the **Store macro in** field, verify that **This Workbook** is selected.
   f) Select the **Description** field, type *Format worksheets* and select **OK**.

g) Observe that the status bar displays a **Stop** button indicating that a macro is currently recording.

2. Format the title of the worksheet.

a) Select cell **A1**.
b) Select **Home→Font→Font Size drop-down arrow** and select **14**.
c) Select **Home→Font→Bold**.
d) Select **Home→Font→Italic**.

3. Format the expense and quarterly headings in column A and row 5.

a) Select the range **A5:A10**, press and hold **Ctrl** and select the range **B5:E5**.
b) Select **Home→Font→Bold**, **Italic**, and **Underline**.

4. Format the quarterly values and totals with currency formatting.

a) Select the range **B6:E10**.
b) Select **Home→Number→Number Format dialog box launcher**.
c) In the **Format Cells** dialog box, select the **Currency** category. Set the **Decimal places** to **zero (0)** and select **OK**.
d) Select cell **A2**.

5. Stop recording the macro.

a) Select View→Macros→Macros drop-down arrow→Stop Recording.

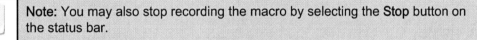

Note: You may also stop recording the macro by selecting the **Stop** button on the status bar.

6. Run the macro on the European worksheet.

a) Select the **European** worksheet.
b) Select **View→Macros→Macros drop-down arrow→View Macros**.
c) In the **Macro** dialog box, verify that the **FormatSheet** macro is selected and select **Run**.

7. Run the macro on the Australian worksheet.

a) Select the **Australian** worksheet.
b) Press **Ctrl+Shift+F**.
c) Verify that the macro runs and the formatting is applied to the Australian worksheet.

	A	B	C	D	E
1	*Develetech Industries - Australian Expenses*				
2					
3	Reported By	Dewey Payne			
4					
5	*Expense*	*Quarter 1*	*Quarter 2*	*Quarter 3*	*Quarter 4*
6	*Fixed expenses*	$228	$427	$165	$105
7	*Flexible expenses*	$464	$485	$197	$478
8	*Discretionary expenses*	$348	$473	$142	$154
9	*Miscellaneous*	$175	$196	$429	$419
10	*Total*	$1,215	$1,581	$933	$1,156

8. Create a macro that clears all formatting.

 a) Select the **North American** worksheet.

 b) Select **View→Macros→Macros drop-down arrow→Record Macro**.

 c) In the **Record Macro** dialog box, in the **Macro name** field, type *ClearFormats* and press **Tab**.

 d) In the **Shortcut key** field, press **Shift+C** to produce the shortcut key **Ctrl+Shift+C**.

 e) In the **Store macro in** field, verify that **This Workbook** is selected.

 f) Select the **Description** field, and type *Clear worksheet formatting* and select **OK**.

9. Record the steps to clear the formatting.

 a) Select the **Select All** button.

 b) Select **Home→Editing→Clear→Clear Formats**.

 c) Press **Ctrl+Home**.

 d) Select **View→Macros→Macros drop-down arrow→Stop Recording**.

10. Save the workbook as a macro-enabled workbook.

 a) Select **File→Save As**.

 b) In the **Backstage** view, in the **Save As** section, select the current folder **Automating Workbook Functionality**.

 c) In the **Save As** dialog box, from the **Save as type** drop-down list, select **Excel Macro-Enabled Workbook (*.xlsm)** and select **Save**.

ACTIVITY 4-4
Editing a Macro

Before You Begin
The workbook **My Regional Expenses.xlsm** is open.

Scenario
While your macro works as you expect, you decide to make a few changes to the formatting. Rather than recording another macro, you decide to edit the macro with the Visual Basic Editor to make the following changes:

* Increase the font size of the worksheet title to 16 points.
* Remove the underlining from the headings in column A and row 5.

---

1. **Open and edit the FormatSheet macro in the Visual Basic Editor.**
   a) Select **View→Macros→Macros drop-down arrow→View Macros**.
   b) In the **Macro** dialog box, verify that the **FormatSheet** macro is selected and select **Edit**.

2. **Edit the macro to change the formatting.**
   a) Maximize the **Visual Basic Editor** and the **My Regional Expenses.xlsm - [Module (Code)]** window.
   b) Below the `Range("A1").Select` statement, in the `With` statement, in the `.Size` line, change the 14 to **16**.

   ```
   Range("A1").Select
   With Selection.Font
       .Name = "Calibri"
       .Size = 16
   ```

3. **Remove the underline formatting from the ranges A5:A10 and B5:E5.**
   a) Below the `Range("A5:A10,B5:E5").Select` statement, in the `Selection.Font.Underline` line, double-click `xlUnderlineStyleSingle` and type *False*

   ```
   Selection.Font.Italic = True
   Selection.Font.Underline = xlUnderlineStyleSingle
   Range("B6:E10").Select
   ```

   b) On the toolbar, select **Save**.
   c) Close the Visual Basic Editor.

4. **Update the formatting on the worksheets using the modified macro.**
   a) Select the **North American** worksheet.
   b) Press **Ctrl+Shift+F**.

c) Verify that the updated macro changes the formatting as expected.

	A	B	C	D	E
1	Develetech Industries - North American Expenses				
2					
3	Reported By	Claire Gibbs			
4					
5	Expense	Quarter 1	Quarter 2	Quarter 3	Quarter 4
6	Fixed expenses	$429	$199	$250	$10,000
7	Flexible expenses	$342	$350	$420	$526
8	Discretionary expenses	$314	$251	$330	$131
9	Miscellaneous	$439	$122	$433	$445
10	Total	$1,524	$922	$1,433	$11,102

d) Apply the macro to the **European** and **Australian** worksheets.

e) Save and close the file.

Summary

In this lesson, you automated workbook functionality to save time and effort and to maintain the data integrity of your workbooks. Even the most well-designed and complex workbooks are useless if you can't trust the data they contain and if users can't or simply don't want to use them. By taking advantage of Excel's automation functionality, you'll be able to relax knowing the analysis you generate from your workbooks provides sound organizational intelligence.

What, if anything, surprised you about the level of automation Excel is capable of?

Can you think of a past task that automation would have made easier, saving you time and effort?

 Note: Check your CHOICE Course screen for opportunities to interact with your classmates, peers, and the larger CHOICE online community about the topics covered in this course or other topics you are interested in. From the Course screen you can also access available resources for a more continuous learning experience.

5 | Creating Sparklines and Mapping Data

Lesson Time: 30 minutes

Lesson Introduction

Often, images can tell a story or provide insight in an instantaneous fashion that isn't always possible with words and numbers. When presenting complex relationships among various bits of data to large groups of people, you may find it easier to display a chart or a map instead of asking the audience to pour over massive amounts of data to see your point.

Fortunately, Microsoft® Office Excel® 2016's capabilities for graphically presenting data go well beyond the use of simple chart types and include mapping data and sparklines. Investing a bit of time now to fully understand what these capabilities are and what they can do will give you the ability to make visual sense of your complex data for nearly any type of presentation or delivery situation.

Lesson Objectives

In this lesson, you will create sparklines and map data. You will:

- Create sparklines.
- Map data.

TOPIC A

Create Sparklines

Although charts and trendlines can be convenient ways to graphically display data, trends, and relationships to worksheet viewers, they aren't always practical. For example, imagine presenting a chart that displays the sales trends for 2,000 sales reps throughout your organization. The chart would be so dense and cluttered, no one would be able to make sense of the information you're presenting. But, it would be nice to give your sales managers an easy way to visually identify trends for any of their reps with just a glance. By taking advantage of Excel's handy data visualization functionality in sparklines, you can combine the benefits of storing massive amounts of data on very large worksheets with the ability to discern important information and identify trends with just a glance.

Sparklines

You can think of *sparklines* as a type of miniature chart that you can actually insert within worksheet cells. Unlike charts, shapes, images, or SmartArt graphics, sparklines are not objects that float above worksheet cells; they become the background image for the cells themselves. You can use sparklines to visually display relative values of cell data over time. Although you can insert sparklines into cells that contain text or data, it is often a good idea, for the sake of legibility, to insert them into empty cells near the data they represent.

You can apply pre-formatted styles to sparklines or customize them to suit your needs. And, you can change the sparkline type for existing sparklines just as you can change chart types. Sparklines can be grouped together so you can apply formatting to large numbers of sparklines simultaneously. As is the case with other cell content such as formulas and functions, you can copy sparklines down a range of data by using relative references to quickly populate large ranges with sparklines. When you create ranges of sparklines all at once or you use the **fill handle** to copy sparklines, Excel automatically groups them together. If you copy and paste sparklines to new cells, Excel does not automatically group them together. You can access the commands for inserting sparklines in the **Sparklines** group on the **Insert** tab.

> **Note:** Be aware that while you can drag the AutoFill handle to copy sparklines to a range, you cannot double-click the AutoFill handle to fill in a range of sparklines.

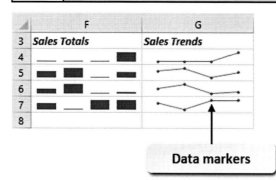

Data markers

Figure 5-1: A worksheet displaying two different types of sparklines.

Sparkline Types

There are three types of sparklines available in Excel 2016: line, column, and win/loss. Each of these sparkline types is best suited to displaying particular types of relationships or trends. The following table describes each of these in some detail.

Sparkline Type	Description
Line 	This sparkline type is ideal for displaying trends in data changes over time. Line style sparklines can also display data markers, which are the points at which the sparkline represents a data entry in the data range.
Column 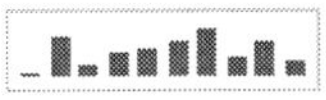	Columns are ideal for showing how the various values in a row of data relate to each other in terms of relative value.
Win/Loss 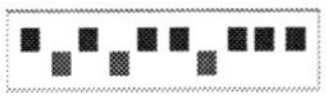	Use the win/loss sparkline type to show which entries are positive and which are negative. The win/loss sparkline does not show relative values among the data points, only which are positive and which are negative.

The Create Sparklines Dialog Box

You will use the **Create Sparklines** dialog box to add sparklines to your worksheets. From here, you can define the data range for your sparklines and select the cells you wish to insert them in. You can access the **Create Sparklines** dialog box by selecting any of the commands in the **Sparklines** group on the **Insert** tab.

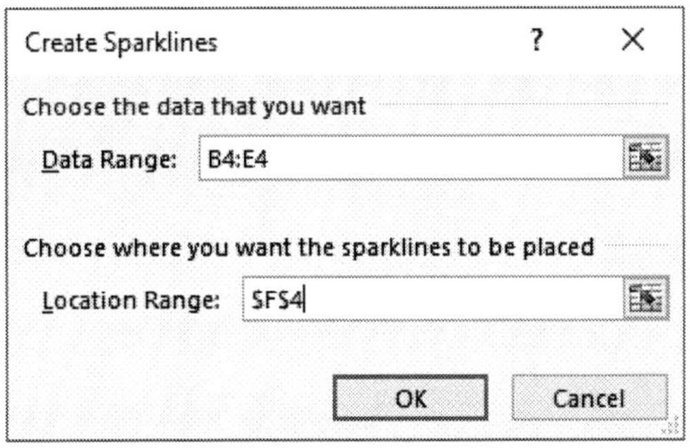

Figure 5-2: Use the Create Sparklines dialog box to add sparklines to worksheet cells.

The Sparkline Tools Contextual Tab

As with many other types of workbook elements, Excel displays the **Sparkline Tools** contextual tab when you select cells that contain sparklines. The **Sparkline Tools** contextual tab contains only one tab, the **Design** tab. The command groups on the **Design** tab display the commands and options you will use to work with sparklines.

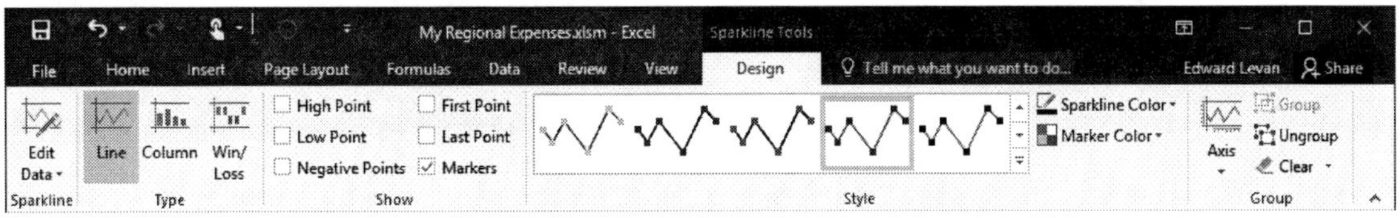

Figure 5-3: The Sparkline Tools contextual tab.

The following table identifies the types of commands you will find in the command groups on the **Design** tab of the **Sparkline Tools** contextual tab.

Design Tab Group	Contains Commands For
Sparkline	Changing the data range associated with sparklines and determining how sparklines handle empty cells in the data range.
Type	Changing sparkline types.
Show	Toggling the display of data markers on and off.
Style	Applying pre-formatted styles or custom formatting to sparklines.
Group	Grouping or ungrouping sparklines, modifying sparkline axes, and removing sparklines from worksheets.

 Access the Checklist tile on your CHOICE Course screen for reference information and job aids on How to Create and Modify Sparklines.

ACTIVITY 5-1
Creating Sparklines

Data File
C:\091057Data\Creating Sparklines and Mapping Data\Develetech Sales.xlsx

Before You Begin
Excel 2016 is open.

Scenario
As sales manager for Develetech Industries, you have been tracking regional sales over the territory. You have built a PivotTable that is configured to show Northeast sales data for each state by month and know that this is a good start to analyze the sales data. You have included some conditional formatting within the PivotTable to see sales above average but decide to include sparklines to see the sales trend for each state.

1. Open the **Develetech Sales.xlsx** workbook.

   a) In Excel, navigate to the **C:\091057Data\Creating Sparklines and Mapping Data** folder and open **Develetech Sales.xlsx**.

   b) Save the file as *My Develetech Sales.xlsx*.

2. Add sales trend sparklines next to the PivotTable.

   a) Verify that the **NE PivotTable** worksheet is selected and that cell **F6** is selected.

   b) Select **Insert→Sparklines→Line**.

   c) In the **Create Sparklines** dialog box, in the **Data Range** field, select the range **B6:D6** and select **OK**.

   ```
   Create Sparklines                    ?    X

   Choose the data that you want

   Data Range:   B6:D6                        ▦

   Choose where you want the sparklines to be placed

   Location Range:  $F$6                      ▦

                  [    OK    ]   [  Cancel  ]
   ```

3. Copy the line sparkline to the other state rows in the PivotTable.

   a) Verify that cell **F6** is selected and AutoFill to cell **F16**.

b) Verify the line sparklines are copied to each of the state rows.

Grand Total	Sales Trends
$699,941.51	
$501,062.76	
$688,847.75	
$770,391.22	
$621,550.62	
$616,402.60	
$649,158.67	
$649,613.96	
$618,355.19	
$627,489.61	
$532,082.01	
$6,974,895.90	

4. Format the line sparklines.

a) Select cell F6.

b) On the **Sparkline Tools** contextual tab, select **Design→Show→Markers** check box.

c) Select **Design→Style→Sparkline Color** and from the menu, select a color of your choice in the **Standard Colors** section.

5. Save the workbook and keep the file open.

TOPIC B

Map Data

Many organizations track data across geographical regions over periods of time. Until Excel 2013, there has been few ways to graphically represent that data. While you can create PivotTables and PivotCharts from the data, there was no method of showing the relationship of that data geographically over time. Fortunately, Excel 2016 now has a built-in feature that does just that, 3D Map.

The 3D Map Feature

The Excel 2016 3D Maps feature allows you to visualize your data on a map by plotting geographic and temporal or time-related data on a 3-D globe or custom map, show it over time, and create visual tours you can share with other people.

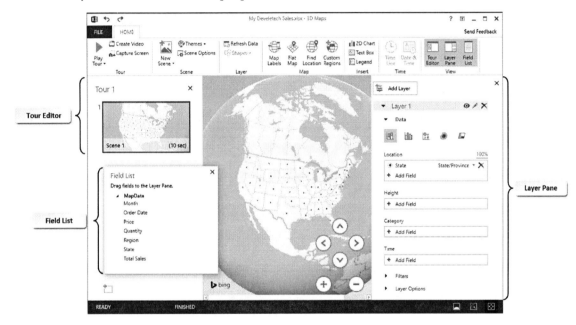

Figure 5-4: 3D Maps.

Data Structuring

For best results with 3D Maps, use data in an Excel table or a Data Model that you created in Excel or by using Power Pivot. Use meaningful headings in your tables for time and geography, which are required, so that 3D Maps can interpret the data correctly. As with all tables, ensure that each row of your data is a complete, unique record in the table. Date or time values should be formatted and labeled appropriately.

> **Note:** See the appendix, Work with Power Pivot, for more details on this topic.

The following table describes the data required to make a 3D Map.

Element	Considerations
Date or time fields	Days, weeks, months, quarters, or years.
	Seconds, minutes, or hours.
Geographic fields	Latitude/Longitude pair, city/state pair, country/region, zip code/ postal code, state/province, or address.

3D Map Elements

In 3D Maps, you can show or hide various components including the **Tour Editor**, the **Layer Pane**, and the **Field List**. The **Layer Pane** is the most critical aspect of working with 3D Maps as it is where you plot your geographical data. The **Tour Editor**, at the left side of the **3D Maps** window shows you the default tour and scene created from your data. A tour is a collection of scenes which can show you time-based relationships between geographic locations and their associated data. The **Field List** displays the fields from your data that can be dragged onto the various sections of the **Layer Pane**.

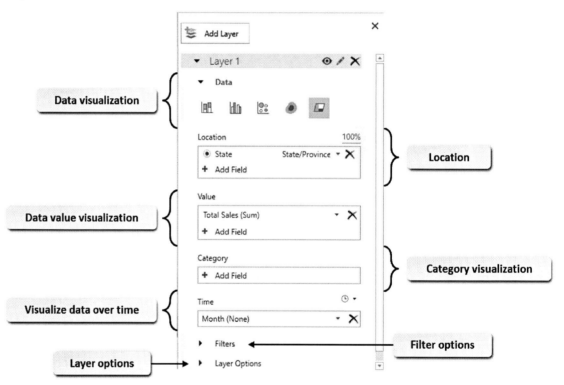

Figure 5-5: 3D Map Layer Pane.

The following table describes the features of the **Layer Pane**.

Data Section	Description
Visualization	Select the visualization from stacked column chart, clustered column chart, bubble chart, heat map, and region visualization.
Location	Add fields for location data.
Height/Size/Value	Add fields for data value visualization.
Category	Add fields for category visualization.
Time	Add fields to visualize data over time.

Data Section	Description
Filters (section)	Add fields to filter your data.
Layer Options (section)	Configure the color, opacity, and values shown in the 3D Map.

Tours

A 3D Maps *tour* can show a time-based relationship between geographic locations and their associated data—such as population numbers, sales values for states, temperature highs or lows, or flight arrival delays. When you start 3D Maps from a workbook that doesn't already contain a tour, a new tour with a single scene is automatically created. You can create tours by selecting **Insert→Tours→3D Map drop-down arrow→Open 3D Maps** and selecting **New Tour** in the **Launch 3D Maps** dialog box. You can also switch between tours and create new tours by using the **Launch 3D Maps** dialog box.

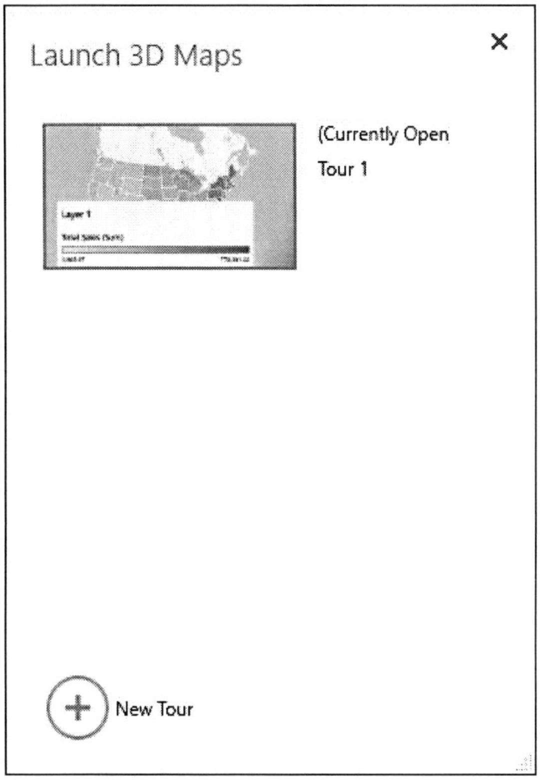

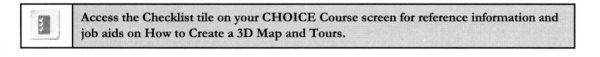

Figure 5–6: Launch 3D Maps dialog box.

Access the Checklist tile on your CHOICE Course screen for reference information and job aids on How to Create a 3D Map and Tours.

ACTIVITY 5-2
Creating a 3D Map

Before You Begin
The file **My Develetech Sales.xlsx** is open.

Scenario
Since you have been tracking regional sales over the territory, you know that a chart will be too crowded with data points. You decide to create a 3D Map to plot the sales for each region as they appear over time.

1. Create a 3D Map.
   a) Select the **Map Data** worksheet.
   b) Verify that a cell in the table is selected.
   c) Select **Insert→Tours→3D Map**.
   d) In the **Microsoft Excel** dialog box indicating that to use this feature enable the data analysis features, select **Enable**.

    Note: It may take a few moments for 3D Maps to activate.

e) In the **3D Maps** window, in the **Layer Pane**, in the **Layer 1** top-level section, in the **Data** subsection, and in the **Location** section, verify that **State** has been identified correctly.

f) In the **Layer Pane**, below the **Data** section header, select the **Region** visualization.

g) In the **Layer Pane**, in the **Value** section, select **Add Field** and choose **Total Sales**.

h) In the **Layer Pane**, in the **Time** section, select **Add Field** and choose **Month**.

2. Add a theme to the scene.

a) Select **HOME→Scene→Themes**.

    b) Select the **Aerial Color** theme, the second theme in the first row.

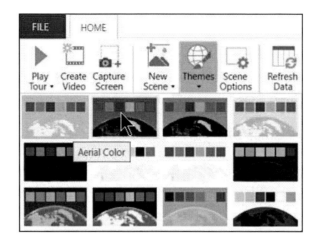

3. Adjust the map and play the scene.

    a) Select **HOME→View→Field List** to turn off the **Field List**.

    b) In the **Layer Pane**, in the **Layer 1** heading, select the **Rename this layer** button.

    c) Select **Layer 1**, type *Develetech Sales* and press **Enter**.

    d) Select the legend and move it to the upper-right of the map.

    e) Shrink the size of the legend by dragging the bottom-right size handle up to remove extra white space.

    f) Select the **Zoom in** button twice.

    g) Select the **Tilt down** button twice.

    h) At the bottom of the **3D Maps** window, on the **Time Line control** bar, select **Play** and observe the data visualization.

4. Close the **3D Maps** window.

a) Select **File→Close**.

5. Save and close the **My Develetech Sales.xlsx** workbook.

Summary

In this lesson, you used sparklines to convey total or trends visually, as well as learned to create a 3D Map from regional and temporal data. Taking advantage of Excel's data visualization functionality will enable you to instantly make a connection with your audience and give workbook viewers instant insight into even the largest datasets.

What is the main benefit of using sparklines over charts or other visual methods to convey meaning from data?

How do you see yourself utilizing the 3D Map feature?

Note: Check your CHOICE Course screen for opportunities to interact with your classmates, peers, and the larger CHOICE online community about the topics covered in this course or other topics you are interested in. From the Course screen you can also access available resources for a more continuous learning experience.

6 | Forecasting Data

Lesson Time: 1 hour, 20 minutes

Lesson Introduction

By now, you're likely well acquainted with creating, building, and maintaining Microsoft® Office Excel® 2016 workbooks and performing all manner of data analysis. When you have all of the data you need and that data is in the correct format, there are practically limitless questions you can use Excel to answer. This is all fine and good when you have a specific question in mind and you're looking for one specific answer. But, what if you want to know how things will change if any number of variables, themselves, change? After all, you can never know for sure just how things will play out in the future. You could simply keep re-entering your data with different values, or you could make numerous copies of your data and update values as needed. But this all takes a lot of time and uses a lot of worksheet real estate to accomplish. And, you'll be saving ever larger workbook files in the process. In short, if you need to crunch your numbers with a variety of different values to anticipate a variety of possible scenarios, you'll want some sort of automated way to do so.

The good news is that Excel contains a robust variety of functionality that is designed to help with such tasks. Becoming familiar with how these different features work and what they can do to help you analyze your data will open whole new worlds of possibilities in terms of data analysis. This can help you with planning, *forecasting*, scheduling, or any number of other tasks that require you to consider the very real possibility that a variety of different outcomes is possible given the unpredictable nature of today's market.

Lesson Objectives

In this lesson, you will forecast data. You will:

- Determine potential outcomes using data tables.

- Determine potential outcomes using scenarios.

- Use the Goal Seek feature.

- Forecast data trends.

TOPIC A

Determine Potential Outcomes Using Data Tables

There are some things in business, as in life, that you just can't predict. It should come as no surprise then that this can makes things a bit tricky when it comes to analyzing your data in order to make predictions about the future. Even when you aren't looking to the future, you may simply need to know what an outcome will be if you change some input in some way. Although there are plenty of ways to do this manually, why would you want to? As you may have guessed by now, the good news is that you simply don't have to.

Excel 2016 includes several features that can help you answer one simple question, "What if?" for a variety of possibilities. What if my interest rate was 7.6 percent instead of 7.4 percent? What if we sell only $3 million worth of product instead of $3.2 million? What if we start the project in May instead of June? How will things change if these variables fluctuate? To get all of the possible answers to questions like this at once, you just need to know how to ask Excel "What if?"

What–If Analysis

When you need to examine multiple possibilities while analyzing a particular dataset, you need to perform what is known in Excel as *what-if analysis*. What-if analysis enables you to perform calculations on the same formula or formulas with one or more variables included at a number of different values. For example, you could calculate your total payment for a car loan based on a variety of different interest rates, or if you put down a variety of different down payments, or both. This enables you to make the best decision possible for your situation based on all of the potential scenarios. Or, let's say you already have a particular outcome in mind: "I can spend a total of $18,000 for this car." How much of a loan can you afford at 5.8 percent interest? Excel can help you figure that out too.

Excel includes three different built-in what-if analysis tools: the Scenario Manager, the Goal Seek feature, and data tables. Each approaches the question "what if?" in a different way. You can access these features by selecting **Data→Forecast→What-If Analysis**.

Figure 6-1: You can perform a variety of different analyses based on varying inputs by using Excel's what-if analysis tools.

Data Tables

The first type of what-if analysis tool we'll look at is *data tables*. Data tables enable you to view a variety of different outcomes for particular formulas or functions given a set of different values for either one or two variables. The main advantage of data tables is that they support any number of values for the variables you are calculating. The main disadvantage is that the more variables you test for, the more space data tables take up; this is because data tables display the results for all variables, or sets of variables, in tabular form.

Each individual data table references at least one formula. The column and/or row labels in a data table represent the values for the one or two variables you wish to calculate on. The variables you wish to change in the formulas or functions must be entered into their own cells, which are known as input cells, and must be included as references to the input cells in the original formulas or functions. When you create the data table, Excel calculates the formula or function results for each variable or set of variables, and then displays the results for each in the data table. As with most other Excel functionality, when you change the other values feeding the formulas or functions, the results automatically update in the data table.

 Caution: Data tables function best when the cells that contain the variables are populated with values instead of formulas. While some data tables function just fine with formulas in the variable cells, you may encounter errors from time to time. If it's easiest to populate the variable cells using formulas, you should consider pasting those results back into the cells as values before creating the data table.

One-Variable Data Tables

Because you can create data tables that calculate formula results for either one or two variables, there are two general types of data tables: one-variable data tables and two-variable data tables. *One-variable data tables* replace the value in one cell, the input cell, with any number of values you choose, plug each of those values into the formulas or functions that reference the input cell, and then display the results in the table next to the row or column label for each corresponding value. Because of the way you must set up data tables on your worksheets, one-variable data tables are the only kind that can replace values for more than one formula or function.

One-variable data tables can be oriented either horizontally or vertically. When they are oriented horizontally, meaning the values for the changing variable are in a single row and serving as column labels, the tables are said to be row-oriented. When data tables are oriented vertically, or with the variable values in a single column serving as row labels, they are said to be column oriented. This is an important distinction because it determines whether you need to enter the input cell reference into the **Row input cell** field or the **Column input cell** field in the **Data Table** dialog box when you create the data table.

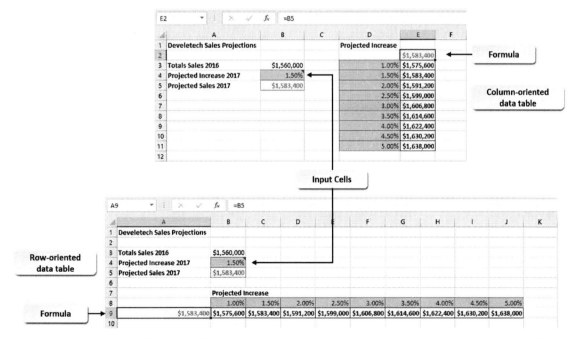

Figure 6-2: One-variable data tables can be column- or row-oriented and can replace a single variable with any number of values for multiple formulas or functions.

Two-Variable Data Tables

Two-variable data tables enable you to replace the values for two different variables in a formula or a function. As with any data table, you can include as many values for each variable as you would like. In contrast with one-variable data tables, you can include only a single formula or function in a two-variable data table. With two-variable data tables, you need two input cells. The values for one of the input cells will be the column labels, and the values for the other input cell will be the row labels. The formula or function referenced by the data table must refer to both input cells.

B9	▾	× ✓ fx	=B6				
	A	B	C	D	E	F	G
1	Develetech Sales Projections						
2							
3	Totals Sales 2016	$1,560,000					
4	Projected Increase 2017	1.50%		**Input cells**			
5	Expenses 2016	10%					
6	Projected Sales 2017	$1,427,400					
7							
8		Projected Increase					
9	**Formula** →	$1,427,400	5%	10%	15%	20%	25%
10		1.00%	$1,497,600	$1,419,600	$1,341,600	$1,263,600	$1,185,600
11		1.50%	$1,505,400	$1,427,400	$1,349,400	$1,271,400	$1,193,400
12		2.00%	$1,513,200	$1,435,200	$1,357,200	$1,279,200	$1,201,200
13		2.50%	$1,521,000	$1,443,000	$1,365,000	$1,287,000	$1,209,000
14		3.00%	$1,528,800	$1,450,800	$1,372,800	$1,294,800	$1,216,800
15		3.50%	$1,536,600	$1,458,600	$1,380,600	$1,302,600	$1,224,600
16		4.00%	$1,544,400	$1,466,400	$1,388,400	$1,310,400	$1,232,400
17		4.50%	$1,552,200	$1,474,200	$1,396,200	$1,318,200	$1,240,200
18		5.00%	$1,560,000	$1,482,000	$1,404,000	$1,326,000	$1,248,000

Figure 6–3: Two-variable data tables allow for more than one variable, but work only on a single formula or function.

The Data Table Dialog Box

You will use the **Data Table** dialog box to define the input cells for your data tables. You enter the cell reference for the input cell containing the value you want to replace with the values in data table column labels in the **Row input cell** field. This may, at first, seem counterintuitive, but remember that column labels all exist within the same row. The opposite is true for the values you have stored in a single column. They serve as row labels, so enter the cell reference for the input cell whose value you want to vary with these in the **Column input cell** field. There is no field to enter the formula or function you are calculating variables for; you will enter it when you create a data table.

Figure 6–4: Use the Data Table dialog box to define your input cells.

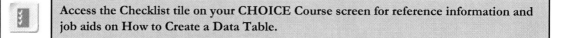

Access the Checklist tile on your CHOICE Course screen for reference information and job aids on How to Create a Data Table.

ACTIVITY 6-1
Determining Potential Outcomes Using Data Tables

Data File
C:\091057Data\Forecasting Data\Develetech Forecasts.xlsx

Before You Begin
Excel 2016 is open.

Scenario
As a member of the accounting department at Develetech Industries, you have been asked to create some what-if scenarios for sales and expense data. You decide to create data tables to substitute the percentages in the calculations that would provide you with what-if scenarios if the percentage rates were to increase or decrease.

---

1. Open the Develetech Forecasts.xlsx workbook.
   a) In Excel, navigate to **C:\091057Data\Forecasting Data** and open the workbook **Develetech Forecasts.xlsx**.
   b) Save the file as *My Develetech Forecasts.xlsx*.

2. Create a one-variable data table to calculate the projected change in sales.

   > **Note:** Cell B4 contains a comment to help with this step in the activity.

   a) Verify that the **Sales** worksheet is selected and that cell **B5** is selected.
   b) Enter the formula *=B3+(B3*B4)*
   c) Select cell **C8** and enter the formula *=B5*
   d) Select the range **B8:C17**, and select **Data→Forecast→What-If Analysis→Data Table**.
   e) In the **Data Table** dialog box, in the **Column input cell** field, select cell **B4** and select OK.

Data Table	?	×
Row input cell:		
Column input cell:	$B$4	
OK		Cancel

   > **Note:** If you select cell **B4**, Excel will automatically treat the cell as an absolute reference.

f) Verify the data table replaced the percentages in the formula creating the projected change of percentage rate.

Develetech Sales Projections		
Totals Sales 2016	$1,560,000	
Projected Increase 2017	1.50%	
Projected Sales 2017	$1,583,400	
	Projected Change	
		$1,583,400
	1.00%	$1,575,600
	1.50%	$1,583,400
	2.00%	$1,591,200
	2.50%	$1,599,000
	3.00%	$1,606,800
	3.50%	$1,614,600
	4.00%	$1,622,400
	4.50%	$1,630,200
	5.00%	$1,638,000

3. Create a two-variable data table to calculate the projected change in sales and expenses.

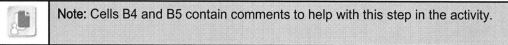 **Note:** Cells B4 and B5 contain comments to help with this step in the activity.

a) Select the **Expenses** worksheet.

b) Verify that cell **B6** is selected and enter the formula *=B3+(B3*B4)-(B3*B5)*

c) Select cell **B9** and enter the formula *=B6*

d) Select the range **B9:G18**, and select **Data→Forecast→What-If Analysis→Data Table**.

e) In the **Data Table** dialog box, select the **Row input cell** field and select cell **B5**.

f) In the **Column input cell** field, select cell **B4** and select **OK**.

Data Table	?	×
Row input cell:	$B$5	
Column input cell:	$B$4	
	OK	Cancel

g) Verify the data table replaced the percentages in the formula for both projected increase and projected expenses.

Develetech Sales Projections						
Totals Sales 2016	$1,560,000					
Projected Increase 2017	1.50%					
Projected Expenses 2017	10%					
Projected Income 2017	$1,427,400					
	Projected Change					
	$1,427,400	5%	10%	15%	20%	25%
	1.00%	$1,497,600	$1,419,600	$1,341,600	$1,263,600	$1,185,600
	1.50%	$1,505,400	$1,427,400	$1,349,400	$1,271,400	$1,193,400
	2.00%	$1,513,200	$1,435,200	$1,357,200	$1,279,200	$1,201,200
	2.50%	$1,521,000	$1,443,000	$1,365,000	$1,287,000	$1,209,000
	3.00%	$1,528,800	$1,450,800	$1,372,800	$1,294,800	$1,216,800
	3.50%	$1,536,600	$1,458,600	$1,380,600	$1,302,600	$1,224,600
	4.00%	$1,544,400	$1,466,400	$1,388,400	$1,310,400	$1,232,400
	4.50%	$1,552,200	$1,474,200	$1,396,200	$1,318,200	$1,240,200
	5.00%	$1,560,000	$1,482,000	$1,404,000	$1,326,000	$1,248,000

4. Save the workbook and keep the file open.

TOPIC B

Determine Potential Outcomes Using Scenarios

Data tables are a convenient way to perform what-if analysis when you need to account for only one or two variables. But what if you need to account for more than two variables? And although convenient, data tables take up a considerable amount of space on worksheets, especially if you include numerous values for the variables. Wouldn't it be nice to be able to perform the same type of analysis for more than two variables, without cluttering your worksheets? This is what the next type of what-if analysis, scenarios, can do.

Scenarios

Scenarios are a type of what-if analysis that enable you to define multiple variables for multiple formulas or functions to determine a variety of outcomes. Unlike data tables, which create new datasets comprising the various calculation results, scenarios change the displayed values of both the cells containing the variables, which are known as changing cells in scenarios, and the cells with the formulas or functions fed by the variables. As you display each scenario, Excel simply replaces the displayed values in place. Another key difference is that, when you create scenarios, Excel converts any formulas or functions in changing cells to values, so you lose the original formulas and functions. For this reason, it is a good idea to make a copy of your original dataset before creating scenarios for it or to include a scenario that represents all of the original values.

You can create any number of scenarios you like for a particular dataset, but each scenario can contain only up to 32 changing values. Any formulas or functions that are fed by the changing cells will update when you display the various scenarios. In addition to displaying various scenarios on your worksheet, you can create a scenario report, which creates a new worksheet that displays the inputs and any specified results of all scenarios.

Scenario Summary	Current Values:	Original	Advertising Campaign
Changing Cells:			
Australia	200,000	200,000	220,000
Canada	130,000	130,000	143,000
Germany	150,000	150,000	165,000
Great_Britain	100,000	100,000	110,000
United_States	300,000	300,000	330,000
Salaries	400,000	400,000	400,000
Rent_Utilities	60,000	60,000	60,000
Advertising	30,000	30,000	40,000
Office_Expenses	9,000	9,000	9,000
Liability_Insurance	200,000	200,000	200,000
Other	5,000	5,000	5,000
Result Cells:			
Total_Revenue	$880,000	$880,000	$968,000
Total_Expenses	$704,000	$704,000	$714,000
Profit	$176,000	$176,000	$254,000

Notes: Current Values column represents values of changing cells at time Scenario Summary Report was created. Changing cells for each scenario are highlighted in gray.

Figure 6–5: A scenario report displaying multiple scenarios.

The Scenario Manager Dialog Box

You will use the **Scenario Manager** dialog box to add scenarios to a worksheet, delete scenarios from a worksheet, edit existing scenarios, create scenario reports, or copy scenarios from other worksheets to the current worksheet. You can access the **Scenario Manager** dialog box by selecting **Data→Forecast→What-If Analysis→Scenario Manager**.

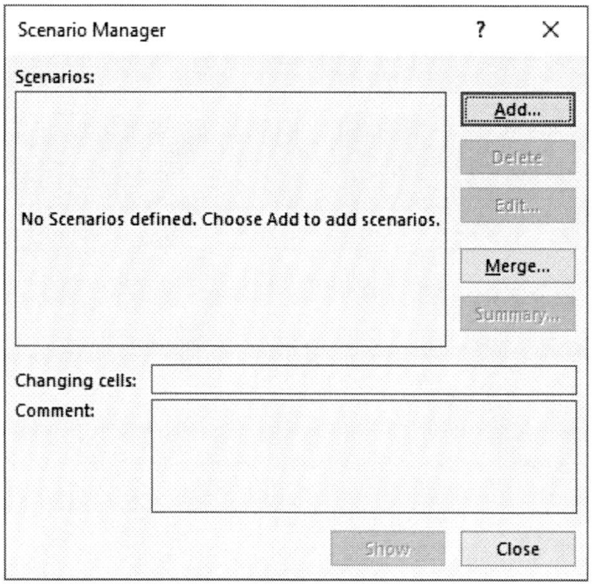

Figure 6-6: The Scenario Manager dialog box.

The following table describes the various elements of the **Scenario Manager** dialog box.

Scenario Manager Dialog Box Element	Description
Scenarios list	Displays all scenarios that have been added to the currently selected worksheet.
Changing cells field	Displays the changing cells for the currently selected scenario in the **Scenarios** list.
Comment field	Displays the ID of the user who created the currently selected scenario, the date the scenario was created, and any comments added by the user who created the scenario.
Add button	Opens the **Add Scenario** dialog box, which enables you to define and add a new scenario to the currently selected worksheet.
Delete button	Deletes the currently selected scenario.
Edit button	Opens the currently selected scenario in the **Edit Scenario** dialog box, which you can use to edit the scenario.
Merge button	Opens the **Merge Scenarios** dialog box, which enables you to merge scenarios from other worksheets and other open workbooks with the currently selected worksheet.
Summary button	Opens the **Scenario Summary** dialog box, which enables you to create a scenario summary report on a new worksheet.
Show button	Shows the results of the currently selected scenario on the currently selected worksheet.
Close button	Closes the **Scenario Manager** dialog box.

The Add Scenario Dialog Box

When you select the **Add** button in the **Scenario Manager** dialog box, Excel opens the **Add Scenario** dialog box. Here, you will define a name and the changing cells for the scenarios you wish to add to your worksheets. You can also set protection formatting options for individual scenarios as you define them.

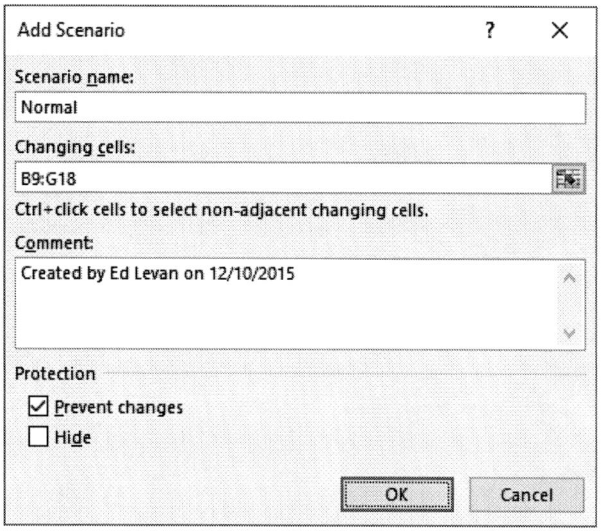

Figure 6-7: Use the Add Scenario dialog box to define new scenarios and apply protection formatting to them.

The following table describes the various elements of the **Add Scenario** dialog box.

Add Scenario Dialog Box Element	Use This To
Scenario name field	Define a name for the scenario.
Changing cells field	View or define the changing cells for the scenario. Whatever cell or range is selected when you create the scenario is displayed here by default.
Comment field	Add comments about the scenario to help other users understand what it's doing.
Prevent changes check box	Prevent other users from editing or showing the scenario. This functionality becomes active only if you also protect the worksheet, which is similar to how cell protection formatting works.
Hide check box	Hide the scenario from view in the **Scenario Manager** dialog box. This functionality becomes active only if you also protect the worksheet, which is similar to how cell protection formatting works.

The Scenario Values Dialog Box

Once you create a scenario, you will use the **Scenario Values** dialog box to define the values for its changing cells. The **Scenario Values** dialog box displays a text field for each of the changing cells you define for the scenario. You can populate these with either numeric values or with formulas. As with nearly all Excel formulas, you must first type an equal sign (=) to use a formula to calculate the value for changing cells. Remember that Excel automatically converts formulas in changing cells to values once you show a scenario on the worksheet.

Once you've defined the values for the changing cells in a scenario, you can either create further scenarios or return to the **Scenario Manager** dialog box. If you select the **Add** button in the **Scenario Values** dialog box, Excel displays the **Add Scenario** dialog box, enabling you to define further scenarios. If you select the **OK** button in the **Scenario Values** dialog box, Excel returns you to the **Scenario Manager** dialog box.

Scenario Values	?	X
Enter values for each of the changing cells.		
1: $B$4	0.015	
2: $B$5	0.1	
Add	OK	Cancel

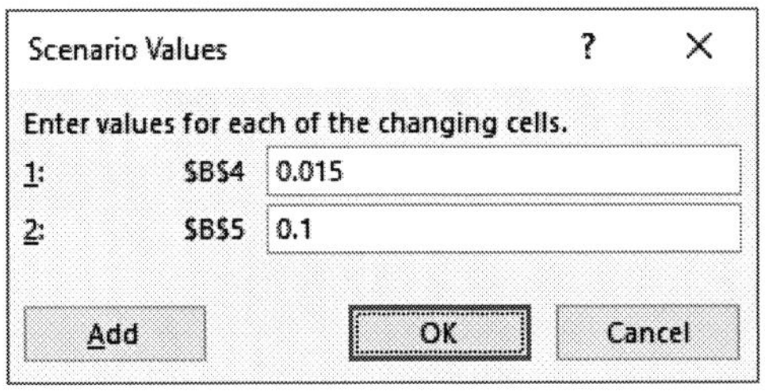

Figure 6-8: Use either hard-coded values or formulas to change the value in scenario changing cells.

The Scenario Command

While you can use the **Scenario Manager** dialog box to show the results of various scenarios on worksheets, Excel provides you with a much more convenient option for doing so: the **Scenario** command. Although it does not appear within the Excel user interface by default, you can add the **Scenario** command to either the **Quick Access Toolbar** or to a custom ribbon group. Selecting the **Scenario** command opens a drop-down menu that displays all defined scenarios for the currently selected worksheet. Selecting any of the scenarios from the drop-down menu will show the results of the scenario in the affected cells.

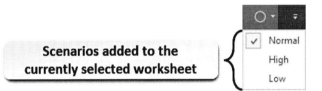

Figure 6-9: Use the Scenario command to quickly switch among scenarios for a worksheet.

> Access the Checklist tile on your CHOICE Course screen for reference information and job aids on How to Work with Scenarios.

ACTIVITY 6-2
Determining Potential Outcomes by Using Scenarios

Before You Begin
The file My Develetech Forecasts.xlsx is open.

Scenario
Continuing your work in the accounting department at Develetech Industries, you have been asked to create some what-if scenarios for projected sales of various countries and company expense data. You have been told to increase the advertising budget to $40,000 and the revenue for each country by 10% for a projected advertising campaign. You decide to create an original scenario as well a scenario for the advertising campaign. In addition, to make each scenario easy to compare, you will create a scenario summary.

---

1. Create a scenario that preserves the original projection values for revenue and expenses.

    a) Select the **Projections** worksheet.
    b) Select the range **B4:B8**. Press and hold **Ctrl** and select the range **B12:B17**.
    c) Select **Data→Forecast→What-If Analysis→Scenario Manager**.
    d) In the **Scenario Manager** dialog box, select **Add**.
    e) In the **Add Scenario** dialog box, in the **Scenario name** field, type *Original*
    f) Observe that the **Changing cells** field shows the range **B4:B8,B12:B17**.
    g) In the **Comment** field, at the end of the default comment text, press **Enter**, and type *Original values* and select **OK**.

    > **Note:** It is good practice to leave the default scenario comment text and add to it, giving you the ability to note who created the scenario and when it was created.

    h) In the **Scenario Values** dialog box, verify that the original values are listed.

    > **Note:** Cell names have been created for each of the scenario values for ease of use for both creating scenarios, and later for use with a scenario summary.

Scenario Values	? X
Enter values for each of the changing cells.	
1: Australia	200000
2: Canada	130000
3: Germany	150000
4: Great_Britain	100000
5: United_States	300000
Add	OK Cancel

   i)   Select **Add**.

2. **Create another scenario for an advertising campaign.**

   a)   In the **Add Scenario** dialog box, in the **Scenario name** field type, *Advertising Campaign*

   b)   In the **Comment** field, at the end of the default comment text, press **Enter**, type *Advertising budget increase to $40,000 and each country's revenue by 10%* and then select **OK**.

   c)   In the **Scenario Values** dialog box, change the values for this scenario as follows:

> **Note:** You may either enter formulas or values in the changing cells.

      • Australia: =200,000*1.1 (220,000)
      • Canada: =130,000*1.1 (143,000)
      • Germany: =150,000*1.1 (165,000)
      • Great_Britain: =100,000*1.1 (110,000)
      • United_States: =300,000*1.1 (330,000)
      • Advertising: 40,000

   d)   Select **OK**.

   e)   In the **Microsoft Excel** dialog box indicating that names and results of formulas were converted into values, select **OK**.

3. **Show the scenarios.**

   a)   In the **Scenario Manager** dialog box, verify that **Advertising Campaign** is selected and select **Show**.

   b)   Observe the changes made to Total Revenue, Total Expenses, and Profit.

9	Total Revenue:	$968,000
10		
11	Expenses	
12	Salaries	400,000
13	Rent/Utilities	60,000
14	Advertising	40,000
15	Office Expenses	9,000
16	Liability Insurance	200,000
17	Other	5,000
18	Total Expenses:	$714,000
19	Profit:	$254,000

   c)   In the **Scenario Manager** dialog box, in the **Scenarios** list box, select **Original** and select **Show**.

4. **Create a scenario summary.**

   a)   In the **Scenario Manager** dialog box, select **Summary**.

   b)   In the **Scenario Summary** dialog box, verify the **Report type** option selected is **Scenario summary**.

   c)   In the **Result cells** field, select **B9**, press and hold **Ctrl** and select cells **B18** and **B19**.

   d)   Select **OK**.

e) Verify the new worksheet **Scenario Summary** is shown.

Scenario Summary		Current Values:	Original	Advertising Campaign
Changing Cells:				
	Australia	200,000	200,000	220,000
	Canada	130,000	130,000	143,000
	Germany	150,000	150,000	165,000
	Great_Britain	100,000	100,000	110,000
	United_States	300,000	300,000	330,000
	Salaries	400,000	400,000	400,000
	Rent_Utilities	60,000	60,000	60,000
	Advertising	30,000	30,000	40,000
	Office_Expenses	9,000	9,000	9,000
	Liability_Insurance	200,000	200,000	200,000
	Other	5,000	5,000	5,000
Result Cells:				
	Total_Revenue	$880,000	$880,000	$968,000
	Total_Expenses	$704,000	$704,000	$714,000
	Profit	$176,000	$176,000	$254,000

Notes: Current Values column represents values of changing cells at time Scenario Summary Report was created. Changing cells for each scenario are highlighted in gray.

5. Save the workbook and keep the file open.

TOPIC C

Use the Goal Seek Feature

Excel provides you with a number of options for determining potential outcomes based on varying inputs. But, suppose you already know the outcome you desire? For example, suppose you need to borrow money to buy a piece of equipment for your business, and you know the total amount you wish to pay back and how long you want to pay on the loan. How do you determine the interest rate you can afford? How would you go about determining which input will result in the desired outcome? Trial and error seems a time-consuming, hit-or-miss proposition.

In addition to the what-if analysis tools that enable you to crunch numbers to arrive at a solution, you can also do the reverse: determine the value of a specific input to arrive at a predetermined outcome. Taking advantage of this functionality means you can avoid manually re-entering values until you achieve the desired result or coming up with complex formulas to perform the calculation for you.

The Goal Seek Feature

The Goal Seek feature is a type of what-if analysis tool that enables you to calculate the value of one input in order to arrive at a specific outcome. This is the opposite of how data tables and scenarios work. You can use the Goal Seek feature to determine the value of a specific input for any formula or function as long as that input can be expressed as a value within a single cell; the Goal Seek feature is capable of calculating for only a single value.

When you run the Goal Seek feature, you must define the set cell—which is the cell that contains the formula or function you want to arrive at the desired value—the value you want for the final outcome, and the changing cell. Excel will calculate the correct value for the changing cell to arrive at the desired value in the set cell. The set cell must contain a formula or a function, and the changing cell must contain a numeric value; it cannot contain a formula or a function.

The Goal Seek Dialog Box

You will use the **Goal Seek** dialog box to define the set cell, the desired outcome value, and the changing cell for your goal. You can access the **Goal Seek** dialog box by selecting **Data→Forecast→What-If Analysis→Goal Seek**.

Goal Seek	?	X
Se̲t cell:	B10	
To va̲lue:	0	
By c̲hanging cell:	$B$3	
	OK	Cancel

Figure 6–10: Use the Goal Seek dialog box to define the conditions for your goal.

Iterative Calculations

The Goal Seek feature is just one of a number of Excel features and functionality that relies on *iterative calculations*. During an iterative calculation, Excel rapidly changes the value of an input or several inputs by a particular increment until it arrives at some specific condition or desired outcome. In the case of using the Goal Seek feature, Excel will continue to replace the value in the changing cell, and then recalculate the formula or function result, until the desired value is achieved.

This is, essentially, the same as a user employing a trial-and-error method for calculating the variable input to achieve the desired goal. The benefit, of course, is that Excel does all the work for you, and does it much, much faster.

 Access the Checklist tile on your CHOICE Course screen for reference information and job aids on How to Use the Goal Seek Feature.

ACTIVITY 6–3
Using the Goal Seek Feature

Before You Begin

The file My Develetech Forecasts.xlsx is open.

Scenario

Since you have been doing an excellent job with the what-if data tables and scenarios, your manager has asked you to discover the break-even point for manufacturing of one of Develetech's products. You decide the best course of action is to use the Goal Seek feature to find out the minimum number of units that need to be sold in order to break even.

---

1. Copy the original data and then discover the break-even point for the manufacturing budget using the Goal Seek feature.

   a) Select the **Break Even** worksheet.
   b) Copy the range **A1:B10** and paste into cell **D1**.
   c) Modify the heading in cell **D1** to **Units Sold to Break Even**.
   d) Select cell **E10**.
   e) Select **Data→Forecast→What-If Analysis→Goal Seek**.
   f) In the **Goal Seek** dialog box, verify that in the **Set cell** field, **E10** is listed.
   g) Select the **To value** field, and type *0*
   h) Select the **By changing cell** field, and select cell **E3**.

   i) Select **OK**.

2. Verify the Goal Seek solution.

a) Observe the units sold cell, **E3** and verify that nearly 300 units must be sold to break even.

	A	B	C	D	E
1	**Manufacturing Budget**			**Units Sold to Break Even**	
2					
3	Units sold	96		Units sold	299.52
4	Price per unit	$5.00		Price per unit	$5.00
5	Total income	$480.00		Total income	$1,497.60
6					
7	Cost per unit	$4.75		Cost per unit	$4.75
8	Overhead	$74.88		Overhead	$74.88
9	Total expenses	$530.88		Total expenses	$1,497.60
10	Profit	($50.88)		Profit	$0.00

Goal Seek Status   ?   ✕

Goal Seeking with Cell E10 found a solution.

Target value: 0
Current value: $0.00

OK   Cancel

b) In the **Goal Seek Status** dialog box, select **OK**.

3. Save the workbook and keep the file open.

TOPIC D

Forecasting Data Trends

Often Excel is used to analyze time-based series data such as sales, server utilization, transactional, or inventory data to find recurring seasonality patterns and trends. In Excel 2016, the new Forecast Sheet feature provides a simple method to help explain your data and predict future trends.

The Forecast Sheet

Excel 2016's new Forecast Sheet feature provides a simple method to take historical date- and/or time-based data to create a visual representation of future data. The **Forecast Sheet** command is located on the **Data** ribbon tab in the **Forecast** group. You may represent the forecast as either a line or column chart. Additionally, you may wish to change some of the advanced settings for your forecast in the **Options** section. The result of using this feature is a new worksheet that shows you projected data to your forecast end in a table and a chart depicting the upper and lower bounds of the forecast.

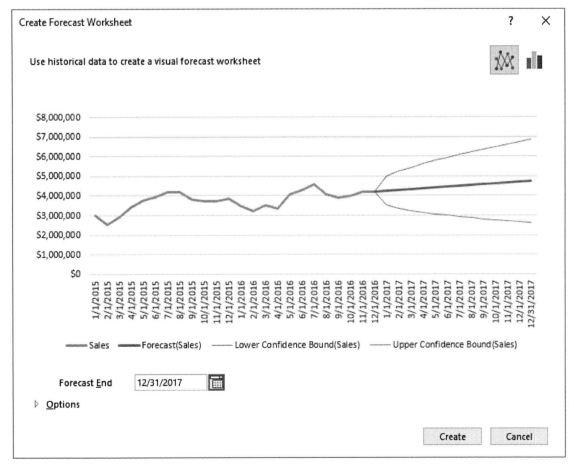

Figure 6-11: The Create Forecast Worksheet Dialog Box.

The following table describes the advanced setting options for the forecast sheet.

Forecast Options	Description
Forecast Start	Select a date for the forecast to begin.

Forecast Options	Description
Confidence Interval	The range surrounding each predicted value in which 95% of future points are expected to fall.
Seasonality	Is automatically detected based on the number of data points of the seasonal pattern.
Timeline Range	The time-based values of your dataset.
Values Range	The values of your dataset.
Fill Missing Points Using	Excel uses interpolation to fill in missing data based on the weighted average of nearby data points.
Aggregate Duplicates Using	Excel averages data that contains the same time stamp.
Include forecast statistics	Select this option to include additional statistical information with the forecast sheet.

 Note: For more information on customizing Excel's language options, access the LearnTO **Build a Histogram Using Analysis ToolPak** presentation from the **LearnTO** tile on the CHOICE Course screen.

 Access the **Checklist** tile on your CHOICE Course screen for reference information and job aids on How to Create a Forecast Sheet.

ACTIVITY 6-4
Forecasting Data with the Forecast Sheet

Before You Begin
The file My Develetech Forecasts.xlsx is open.

Scenario
As part of your what-if analysis, your manager has asked you to provide a forecast of monthly sales data. You have been given sales data from 2015 through 2016 and want to forecast through 12/31/2017. You decide to use the Forecast Sheet feature to project sales for the next year.

1. Create a forecast sheet from monthly sales data.
   a) Select the **Sales Data** worksheet.
   b) Verify that the worksheet contains sales data for 2015 and 2016.
   c) Press **Ctrl+A** to select all the sales data.
   d) Select **Data→Forecast→Forecast Sheet**.

   e) In the **Create Forecast Worksheet** dialog box, verify that the **Create a line chart** option ⁂ is selected.
   f) In the **Forecast End** date selector, choose **12/31/2017**.

   g) Select **Create**.

2. Explore the new forecast worksheet.

   a) Observe that the new worksheet contains a line chart and a table forecasting sales for 2017.

   b) Scroll down the worksheet to see the forecast sales for the year 2017.

	Date	Sales	Forecast(Sales)	Lower Confidence Bound(Sales)	Upper Confidence Bound(Sales)
25	12/1/2016	$4,209,878	$4,209,878	$4,209,878	$4,209,878
26	1/1/2017		$4,251,867	$3,497,987	$5,005,746
27	2/1/2017		$4,293,855	$3,351,053	$5,236,657
28	3/1/2017		$4,335,844	$3,235,720	$5,435,967
29	4/1/2017		$4,377,832	$3,139,881	$5,615,783
30	5/1/2017		$4,419,821	$3,057,606	$5,782,035
31	6/1/2017		$4,461,809	$2,985,464	$5,938,154
32	7/1/2017		$4,503,798	$2,921,263	$6,086,333
33	8/1/2017		$4,545,786	$2,863,496	$6,228,077
34	9/1/2017		$4,587,775	$2,811,080	$6,364,470
35	10/1/2017		$4,629,763	$2,763,202	$6,496,325
36	11/1/2017		$4,671,752	$2,719,235	$6,624,269
37	12/1/2017		$4,713,740	$2,678,684	$6,748,797
38	12/31/2017		$4,754,375	$2,642,311	$6,866,438

   c) Rename the worksheet **Sales Forecast**.

3. Save the workbook, close the file, and exit Excel.

Summary

In this lesson, you used a variety of Excel's automated data analysis tools to gain insight into raw data. Excel's built-in analysis capabilities can save you incredible amounts of time and effort. By using these tools, you can avoid repetitious entry of data with different variable values to determine specific outcomes and perform complex data analysis in a few simple steps. You can also account for a great variety of variable values and given constraints to determine the ideal steps to take in any number of different situations.

How will you be able to use what-if analysis right away when you return to your daily tasks?

How will you be able to use the Forecast Sheet feature for future data analysis?

> **Note:** Check your CHOICE Course screen for opportunities to interact with your classmates, peers, and the larger CHOICE online community about the topics covered in this course or other topics you are interested in. From the Course screen you can also access available resources for a more continuous learning experience.

Course Follow-Up

Congratulations! You have completed the *Microsoft® Office Excel® 2016: Part 3* course. You have successfully worked with a number of different workbooks simultaneously, used Lookup functions and audited formulas, collaborated with colleagues to develop workbooks, automated a variety of tasks, and visually represented data in various formats, as well as determined or predicted what-if or future values using Excel's what-if analysis tools.

Remaining competitive in today's market requires constant vigilance and a continual effort to look forward, which means you can't let distractions get in the way. You can't afford to get bogged down in continuous review cycles or back-and-forth communications. You don't have the time to constantly perform repetitive, low-value tasks just to maintain your workbooks. When problems arise, you need to solve them quickly. By letting Excel do this kind of heavy lifting for you, you will free yourself from time-consuming tasks that keep your focus off of analyzing your data to help organizational leaders make informed, beneficial decisions.

What's Next?

You are encouraged to take the Logical Operations courses *Microsoft® Office Excel ®2016: Data Analysis with PivotTables* and *Microsoft® Office Excel® 2016: Data Analysis with Power Pivot* to dive deeper into the powerful Excel features you've been introduced to throughout this course series. Likewise, continue building upon your Excel knowledge and experience by seeking out other sources to hone and expand your skill set. Participate in online forums and user groups to discover new ways to construct Excel formulas and functions to tackle difficult tasks. Research available add-ins and other support tools to help you get the most out of your Excel experience. And search for online videos and tutorials that demonstrate how to resolve common issues users experience. You are also encouraged to explore Excel further by actively participating in any of the social media forums set up by your instructor or training administrator through the **Social Media** tile on the CHOICE Course screen.

A | Microsoft Office Excel 2016 Exam 77-727

Selected Logical Operations courseware addresses Microsoft Office Specialist (MOS) certification skills for Microsoft® Office Excel® 2016. The following table indicates where Excel 2016 skills that are tested on Exam 77-727 are covered in the Logical Operations Excel 2016 series of courses.

Objective Domain	Covered In
1. Create and Manage Worksheets and Workbooks	
1.1 Create Worksheets and Workbooks	
1.1.1 Create a workbook	Part 1
1.1.2 Import data from a delimited text file	Part 3, Appendix E
1.1.3 Add a worksheet to an existing workbook	Part 1
1.1.4 Copy and move a worksheet	Part 1
1.2 Navigate in Worksheets and Workbooks	
1.2.1 Search for data within a workbook	Part 1
1.2.2 Navigate to a named cell, range, or workbook element	Part 2
1.2.3 Insert and remove hyperlinks	Part 1
1.3 Format Worksheets and Workbooks	
1.3.1 Change worksheet tab color	Part 1
1.3.2 Rename a worksheet	Part 1
1.3.3 Change worksheet order	Part 1
1.3.4 Modify page setup	Part 1
1.3.5 Insert and delete columns or rows	Part 1
1.3.6 Change workbook themes	Part 1
1.3.7 Adjust row height and column width	Part 1
1.3.8 Insert headers and footers	Part 1
1.4 Customize Options and Views for Worksheets and Workbooks	
1.4.1 Hide or unhide worksheets	Part 1
1.4.2 Hide or unhide columns and rows	Part 1
1.4.3 Customize the Quick Access Toolbar	Part 1

Objective Domain	Covered In
1.4.4 Change workbook views	Part 1
1.4.5 Change window views	Part 1
1.4.6 Modify document properties	Part 1
1.4.7 Change magnification by using zoom tools	Part 1
1.4.8 Display formulas	Part 3, Appendix H
1.5 Configure Worksheets and Workbooks for Distribution	
1.5.1 Set a print area	Part 1
1.5.2 Save workbooks in alternative file formats	Part 1; Part 3, Topic 3-A
1.5.3 Print all or part of a workbook	Part 1
1.5.4 Set print scaling	Part 1
1.5.5 Display repeating row and column titles on multipage worksheets	Part 1
1.5.6 Inspect a workbook for hidden properties or personal information	Part 3, Topic 3-B
1.5.7 Inspect a workbook for accessibility issues	Part 3, Topic 3-A
1.5.8 Inspect a workbook for compatibility issues	Part 1
2. Manage Data Cells and Ranges	
2.1 Insert Data in Cells and Ranges	
2.1.1 Replace data	Part 1
2.1.2 Cut, copy, or paste data	Part 1
2.1.3 Paste data by using special paste options	Part 1
2.1.4 Fill cells by using AutoFill	Part 1
2.1.5 Insert and delete cells	Part 1
2.2 Format Cells and Ranges	
2.2.1 Merge cells	Part 1
2.2.2 Modify cell alignment and indentation	Part 1
2.2.3 Format cells by using Format Painter	Part 1
2.2.4 Wrap text within cells	Part 1
2.2.5 Apply number formats	Part 1
2.2.6 Apply cell formats	Part 1
2.2.7 Apply cell styles	Part 1
2.3 Summarize and Organize Data	
2.3.1 Insert sparklines	Part 3, Topic 5-A
2.3.2 Outline data	Part 2
2.3.3 Insert subtotals	Part 2
2.3.4 Apply conditional formatting	Part 2; Part 1

Objective Domain	Covered In
3. Create Tables	
3.1 Create and Manage Tables	
3.1.1 Create an Excel table from a cell range	Part 2
3.1.2 Convert a table to a cell range	Part 2
3.1.3 Add or remove table rows and columns	Part 2
3.2 Manage Table Styles and Options	
3.2.1 Apply styles to tables	Part 2
3.2.2 Configure table style options	Part 2
3.2.3 Insert total rows	Part 2
3.3 Filter and Sort a Table	
3.3.1 Filter records	Part 2
3.3.2 Sort data by multiple columns	Part 2
3.3.3 Change sort order	Part 2
3.3.4 Remove duplicate records	Part 2
4. Perform Operations with Formulas and Functions	
4.1 Summarize Data by Using Functions	
4.1.1 Insert references	Part 1
4.1.2 Perform calculations by using the SUM function	Part 1
4.1.3 Perform calculations by using MIN and MAX functions	Part 1
4.1.4 Perform calculations by using the COUNT function	Part 1
4.1.5 Perform calculations by using the AVERAGE function	Part 1
4.2 Perform Conditional Operations by Using Functions	
4.2.1 Perform logical operations by using the IF function	Part 2
4.2.2 Perform logical operations by using the SUMIF function	Part 2
4.2.3 Perform logical operations by using the AVERAGEIF function	Part 2
4.2.4 Perform statistical operations by using the COUNTIF function	Part 2
4.3 Format and Modify Text by Using Functions	
4.3.1 Format text by using the RIGHT, LEFT, and MID functions	Part 2
4.3.2 Format text by using the UPPER, LOWER, and PROPER functions	Part 2
4.3.3 Format text by using the CONCATENATE function	Part 2
5. Create Charts and Objects	

Objective Domain	Covered In
5.1 Create Charts	
5.1.1 Create a new chart	Part 2
5.1.2 Add additional data series	Part 2
5.1.3 Switch between rows and columns in source data	Part 2
5.1.4 Analyze data by using Quick Analysis	Part 2
5.2 Format Charts	
5.2.1 Resize charts	Part 2
5.2.2 Add and modify chart elements	Part 2
5.2.3 Apply chart layouts and styles	Part 2
5.2.4 Move charts to a chart sheet	Part 2
5.3 Insert and Format Objects	
5.3.1 Insert text boxes and shapes	Part 2
5.3.2 Insert images	Part 2
5.3.3 Modify object properties	Part 2
5.3.4 Add alternative text to objects for accessibility	Part 2

B | Microsoft Office Excel 2016 Expert Exam 77-728

Selected Logical Operations courseware addresses Microsoft Office Specialist (MOS) certification skills for Microsoft® Office Excel® 2016. The following table indicates where Excel 2016 skills that are tested on Exam 77–728 are covered in the Logical Operations Excel 2016 series of courses.

Objective Domain	Covered In
1. Manage Workbook Options and Settings	
1.1. Manage Workbooks	
1.1.1 Save a workbook as a template	Part 1
1.1.2 Copy macros between workbooks	Part 3, Topic 4-C
1.1.3 Reference data in another workbook	Part 3, Topic 1-A
1.1.4 Reference data by using structured references	Part 2
1.1.5 Enable macros in a workbook	Part 3, Topic 4-C
1.1.6 Display hidden ribbon tabs	Part 1
1.2 Manage Workbook Review	
1.2.1 Restrict editing	Part 3, Topic 3-B
1.2.2 Protect a worksheet	Part 3, Topic 3-B
1.2.3 Configure formula calculation options	Part 2
1.2.4 Protect workbook structure	Part 3, Topic 3-B
1.2.5 Manage workbook versions	Part 1
1.2.6 Encrypt a workbook with a password	Part 3, Topic 3-B
2. Apply Custom Data Formats and Layouts	
2.1 Apply Custom Data Formats	
2.1.1 Create custom number formats	Part 1
2.1.2 Populate cells by using advanced Fill Series options	Part 1
2.1.3 Configure data validation	Part 3, Topic 4-A
2.2 Apply Advanced Conditional Formatting and Filtering	

Objective Domain	Covered In
2.1.1 Create custom conditional formatting rules	Part 2
2.2.2 Create conditional formatting rules that use formulas	Part 2
2.2.3 Manage conditional formatting rules	Part 2
2.3 Create and Modify Custom Workbook Elements	
2.3.1 Create custom color formats	Part 1
2.3.2 Create and modify cell styles	Part 1
2.3.3 Create and modify custom themes	Part 1
2.3.4 Create and modify simple macros	Part 3, Topic 4-C
2.3.5 Insert and configure form controls	Part 3, Appendix I
2.4 Prepare a Workbook for Internationalization	
2.4.1 Display data in multiple international formats	Part 3, Appendix F
2.4.2 Apply international currency formats	Part 3, Appendix F
2.4.3 Manage multiple options for +Body and +Heading fonts	Part 3, Appendix F
3. Create Advanced Formulas	
3.1 Apply Functions in Formulas	
3.1.1 Perform logical operations by using AND, OR, and NOT functions	Part 2
3.1.2 Perform logical operations by using nested functions	Part 2
3.1.3 Perform statistical operations by using SUMIFS, AVERAGEIFS, and COUNTIFS functions	Part 2
3.2 Look Up Data by Using Functions	
3.2.1 Look up data by using the VLOOKUP function	Part 3, Topic 2-A
3.2.2 Look up data by using the HLOOKUP function	Part 3, Topic 2-A
3.2.3 Look up data by using the MATCH function	Part 3, Topic 2-A
3.2.4 Look up data by using the INDEX function	Part 3, Topic 2-A
3.3 Apply Advanced Date and Time Functions	
3.3.1 Reference the date and time by using the NOW and TODAY functions	Part 2
3.3.2 Serialize numbers by using date and time functions	Part 2
3.4 Perform Data Analysis and Business Intelligence	
3.4.1 Import, transform, combine, display, and connect to data	Part 3, Topics 1-A, 1-B, Appendix E
3.4.2 Consolidate data	Part 3, Topic 1-C
3.4.3 Perform what-if analysis by using Goal Seek and Scenario Manager	Part 3, Topics 6-B, 6-C
3.4.4 Use cube functions to get data out of the Excel data model	Part 3, Appendix D
3.4.5 Calculate data by using financial functions	Part 2

Objective Domain	Covered In
3.5 Troubleshoot Formulas	
3.5.1 Trace precedence and dependence	Part 3, Topic 2-B
3.5.2 Monitor cells and formulas by using the Watch Window	Part 3, Topic 2-C
3.5.3 Validate formulas by using error checking rules	Part 3, Topic 4-B
3.5.4 Evaluate formulas	Part 3, Topic 2-C
3.6 Define Named Ranges and Objects	
3.6.1 Name cells	Part 2
3.6.2 Name data ranges	Part 2
3.6.3 Name tables	Part 2
3.6.4 Manage named ranges and objects	Part 2
4. Create Advanced Charts and Tables	
4.1 Create Advanced Charts	
4.1.1 Add trendlines to charts	Part 2
4.1.2 Create dual-axis charts	Part 2
4.1.3 Save a chart as a template	Part 2
4.2 Create and Manage PivotTables	
4.2.1 Create PivotTables	Part 2
4.2.2 Modify field selections and options	Part 2
4.2.3 Create slicers	Part 2
4.2.4 Group PivotTable data	Part 2
4.2.5 Reference data in a PivotTable by using the GETPIVOTDATA function	Part 2
4.2.6 Add calculated fields	Part 3, Appendix G
4.2.7 Format data	Part 2
4.3 Create and Manage PivotCharts	
4.3.1 Create PivotCharts	Part 2
4.3.2 Manipulate options in existing PivotCharts	Part 2
4.3.3 Apply styles to PivotCharts	Part 2
4.3.4 Drill down into PivotChart details	Part 2

C | Microsoft Excel 2016 Common Keyboard Shortcuts

The follow table lists common keyboard shortcuts you can use in Microsoft® Office Excel® 2016.

Function	Shortcut
Switch between worksheet tabs, from left to right.	**Ctrl+PgDn**
Switch between worksheet tabs, from right to left.	**Ctrl+PgUp**
Select the region around the active cell (requires there to be content in the surrounding cells).	**Ctrl+Shift+*** or **Ctrl+*** (from the number pad)
Select the cell at the beginning of the worksheet or pane.	**Ctrl+Home**
Select the cell at the end of the worksheet.	**Ctrl+End**
Select the cell at an edge of the worksheet.	**Ctrl+Arrow keys**
Insert the current time.	**Ctrl+Shift+:**
Insert the current date.	**Ctrl+;**
Display the **Insert** dialog box.	**Ctrl+Shift++**
Display the **Delete** dialog box.	**Ctrl+-**
Display the **Format Cells** dialog box.	**Ctrl+1**
Select the entire worksheet.	**Ctrl+A**
Apply or remove bold formatting.	**Ctrl+B**
Apply or remove italic formatting.	**Ctrl+I**
Copy the selected cells.	**Ctrl+C**
Cut the selected cells.	**Ctrl+X**
Paste copied content.	**Ctrl+V**
Display the **Find and Replace** dialog box.	**Ctrl+F**
Display the **Insert Hyperlink** or **Edit Hyperlink** dialog box.	**Ctrl+K**

Function	Shortcut
Create a new workbook.	**Ctrl+N**
Close an open workbook.	**Ctrl+W**
Display the **Open** tab on the **Backstage** view.	**Ctrl+O**
Display the **Print** tab on the **Backstage** view.	**Ctrl+P**
Save the file.	**Ctrl+S**
Repeat the last command or action, if possible.	**Ctrl+Y** or **F4** (when the insertion point is not in the **Formula Bar**)
Undo the last command or action.	**Ctrl+Z**
Redo the last undo.	**Ctrl+Y**
Enter data in a cell while keeping it the active cell.	**Ctrl+Enter**
Select all contiguously populated cells in a column from the selected cell to the end of the range.	**Ctrl+Shift+Up Arrow** or **Ctrl+Shift+Down Arrow**
Select all contiguously populated cells in a row from the selected cell to the end of the range.	**Ctrl+Shift+Right Arrow** or **Ctrl+Shift+Left Arrow**
Toggle among relative, absolute, and mixed references when the insertion point is in or next to a cell reference in the **Formula Bar**.	**F4**
Open the **Save As** dialog box.	**F12**
Activate the **Tell Me** text box.	**Alt+Q**

D | Cube Functions

Microsoft® Office Excel® 2016 includes a set of functions called cube functions that you can use to query data stored in certain databases. Cube functions are designed to work with Online Analytical Processing (OLAP) databases. OLAP databases differ from relational databases, such as Microsoft® Access®, in that they store data, relationships, and hierarchies in multidimensional structures known as cubes instead of in two-dimensional tables. Using data from OLAP database sources speeds up the process of querying data because the server hosting the database, not Excel, does a lot of the processing for you. When you import data into a workbook from an OLAP database, Excel brings it in as a PivotTable or a PivotChart.

 Note: An in-depth discussion on OLAP databases and cubes is beyond the scope of this course. For more information on these topics, please visit **office.microsoft.com**.

Excel 2016 includes seven cube functions you can use to query data stored in OLAP databases.

Function	Description	Syntax
CUBEKPIMEMBER	Returns a key performance indicator (KPI) property and displays the KPI name in the cell.	=CUBEKPIMEMBER(con nection, kpi_name, kpi_property, [caption])
CUBEMEMBER	Will help identify whether or not a particular member belongs to a cube.	=CUBEMEMBER(connecti on, member_expression, [caption])
CUBEMEMBERPROPE RTY	Takes the CUBEMEMBER function one step further and returns a specific property value for the specified member if it exists in the cube.	=CUBEMEMBERPROPER TY(connection, member_expression, property)
CUBERANKEDMEMBE R	Returns the specified ranked members of a cube set. This can be useful for identifying top- or bottom-performers from within the database.	=CUBERANKEDMEMBE R(connection, set_expression, rank, [caption])
CUBESET	Defines a calculated set of members.	=CUBESET(connection, set_expression, [caption], [sort_order], [sort_by])
CUBESETCOUNT	Returns the number of items in a set.	=CUBESETCOUNT(set)

Function	Description	Syntax
CUBEVALUE	Returns a single or combined value from the cube.	=CUBEVALUE(connection, [member_expression1], [member_expression2], …)

 # Importing and Export Data

Appendix Introduction

In this appendix, you'll learn more about importing and exporting data.

TOPIC A

Import and Export Data

Although Microsoft® Office Excel® 2016 is quite handy for entering and analyzing vast amounts of data, entering data you already have readily available in another source is, quite frankly, a waste of time. Copying or re-entering data from Excel worksheets to external applications or databases is a waste of time as well. So, Excel 2016 enables you to import data to or export data from your workbooks. Doing so can not only save you incredible amounts of time and effort, but it can also help eliminate errors that could be introduced by manually transferring information.

Importing and Exporting

Importing is the process of bringing information or data into an application or database from an outside source. Exporting is the process of sending information out of an application or database to another. Excel 2016 enables you to import data from and export data to a number of other applications and database types. You can access the commands for importing data from outside sources in the **Get External Data** group on the **Data** ribbon tab. You can access the commands for exporting data in a number of different formats by selecting **File→Export**.

There are several sources from which you can import data into Excel. The following table describes the three most common ones.

Data Source	Description
Access databases	Excel enables you to import data from any of the tables in Microsoft® Access® databases to which you have access.
The web	Web queries enable you to import data from pages on the World Wide Web. One of the key benefits of this feature is that, as the data updates on the websites, Excel automatically updates the information in your workbooks as well. You can use web queries to import a specific table, multiple tables, or all of the text on a given page.
Text files	This option enables you to import data from simple text files that are delimited in a variety of ways.

There are also four common formats for exporting Excel data for use in other applications. These are described in the following table.

Export Option	Description
Text (Tab delimited) (*.txt)	Exports Excel data as a tab-delimited text file. In these files, individual entries are separated by pressing the **Tab** key.
CSV (Comma delimited) (*.csv)	Exports Excel data as a comma-delimited text file. Individual entries are defined by placing a comma between them.
Formatted Text (Space delimited) (*.prn)	Exports Excel data as a space-delimited text file. These are similar to tab-delimited text files, but they use a single space between characters to define individual entries.
PDF/XPS document	This option doesn't technically export Excel data, but rather saves documents in either the Portable Document Format (PDF) or XML Paper Specification (XPS) format so they can be opened and viewed in other applications, such as Adobe® Acrobat® and Adobe Reader® or an XPS viewer built in to Windows.

Methods of Importing Text Files

There are two methods you can use to import data from text files into Excel. You can either open the text file within Excel or you can import the data from the text file as a data range. If you open the file directly in Excel, you do not need to create a link to the text file. If you import the data, you will need to link the workbook to the text file in order for changes to the text file to reflect in the Excel workbook. Not all text file formats are directly compatible with Excel, so you may not be able to open all text files directly in Excel.

The Text Import Wizard

You will use the **Text Import Wizard** to configure the importation of data from text files. The **Text Import Wizard** walks you through a three-step process in which you identify the type of data the file contains and where you would like to start the import; select the type of character that separates entries in delimited files; and then select the desired cell formatting options for the columns that will contain the data after importing. Each step of the wizard displays a preview of what the imported text will look like given the current selections and settings. You can access the **Text Import Wizard** two ways: by opening a text file from **File→Open** or by selecting **Data→Get External Data→From Text**, and then selecting the desired text document in the **Import Text File** dialog box.

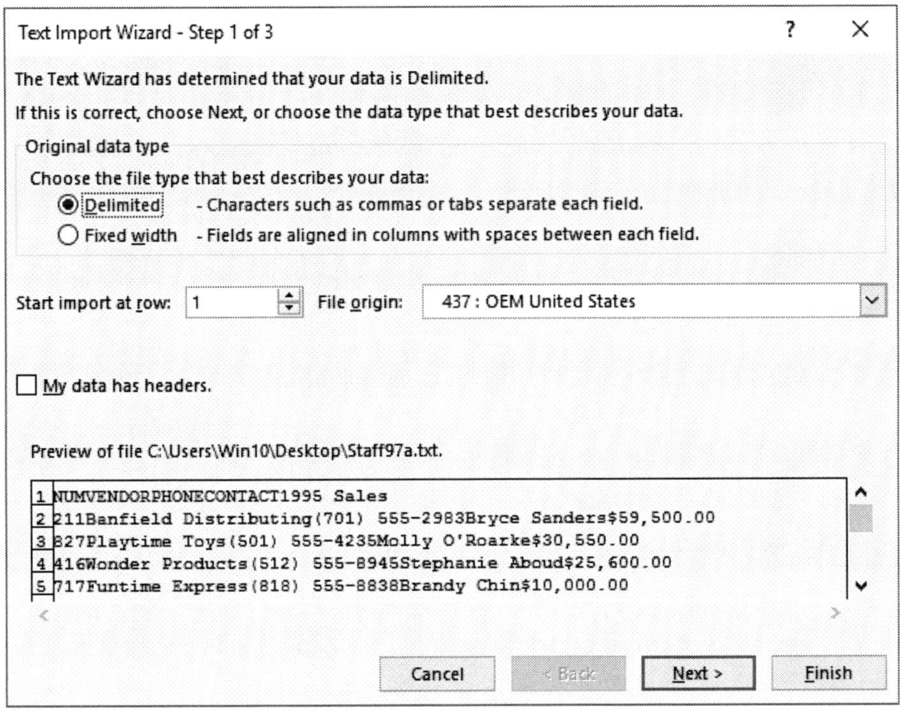

Figure E-1: The Text Import Wizard.

The New Web Query Dialog Box

When you import data from the web, Excel opens the **New Web Query** dialog box. From here, you can navigate to the web page from which you wish to import data and select the specific data you wish to import. Selecting the yellow and black arrow icons [image] selects either particular tables or screen elements, or the entire page for importation. You can access the **New Web Query** dialog box by selecting **Data→Get External Data→From Web**.

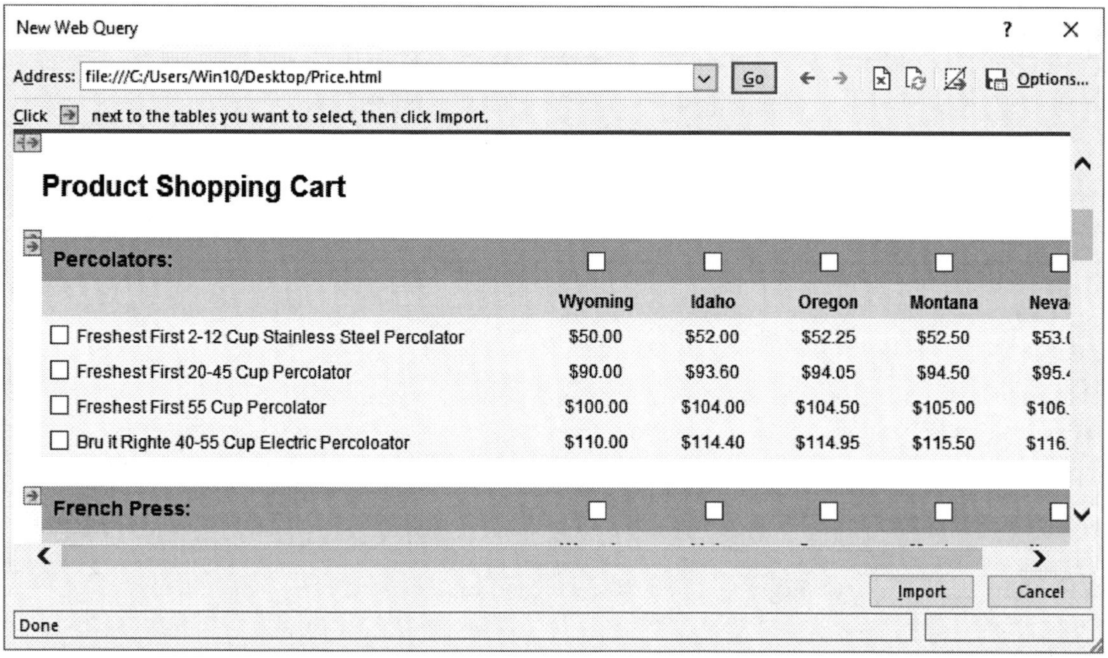

Figure E-2: The New Web Query dialog box.

> [!NOTE]
> **Access the Checklist tile on your CHOICE Course screen for reference information and job aids on How to Import and Export Data.**

XML

The eXtensible Markup Language, or XML, is a computer language that describes data by using structured text files. XML elements are contained within tags that hold the actual data. Once these tags have been defined, data can be moved and exchanged between and among XML-compatible applications. XML is compatible with a large number of applications, making it an ideal format for data exchange.

XML Schemas

An XML schema establishes the rules and structure for other XML files. You must set out the data type and allowable attributes of XML files in a schema. One schema can provide the structure for multiple other XML files. Schemas can outline a particular structural hierarchy for the data in an XML document, as well as define the types of data that exist within the document. Schema files are saved with the .xsd file extension.

You use XML tags to define the data types that exist within a schema. For example, in the source XML file that you want to import, your data entries might contain tags that look like this: <LastName>Smith</LastName>, <FirstName>Bob</FirstName>, and <MiddleInitial>L</MiddleInitial>. In your XML schema file, you would include these tag sets to define data types the schema will recognize. Once you have these data types defined for your entries, which is the text inside the tags, you can create column labels on the target worksheet to match: Last Name, First Name, and MI. Then you simply need to tell Excel which data type goes in which column for the import. This process is known as mapping.

XML Maps

You create maps in Excel to tell it where to put particular data types from an XML document in your worksheets. Excel uses the structure defined within the XML schema file to identify where entries should be placed. Each unique data type, as defined by the schema tags, appears as a separate element in XML maps. To tell Excel where to place entries for that particular element, you simply drag the map element to the desired spreadsheet location. The cells you map the content to represent the starting points for particular types of data to import to. Typically, this would be the first cell in a particular column below the column label.

One of the key things to remember about XML schema files you are using as maps is that the schema file does not contain the data you will ultimately import into Excel. The data will be contained in a separate XML file that uses the tags defined in the schema file to identify data types. Wherever you map a particular data type to on a worksheet is the cell that entries contained within the same set of tags in the data source document will begin populating during the import. Subsequent entries within the same tags will populate down the column by default.

The XML Source Task Pane

You can use the **XML Source** task pane to map elements of an XML schema to the desired worksheet cells. From here, you can add XML schema files to a workbook to use as maps, set mapping options, and map schema elements to the desired locations. For the currently selected map, the **XML Source** task pane displays all unique elements, which you can manually drag to the cell you want that data type to start importing to. You can access the **XML Source** task pane by selecting **Developer→XML→Source**.

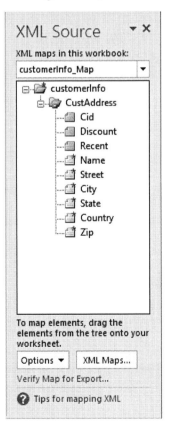

Figure E-3: The XML Source task pane.

The XML Maps Dialog Box

You can use the **XML Maps** dialog box to add, delete, or rename XML maps in your workbook files. The **XML Maps** dialog box displays a list of all maps attached to the currently selected workbook. You can have more than one XML map attached to a workbook file simultaneously. To access the **XML Maps** dialog box, select **XML Maps** in the **XML Source** task pane.

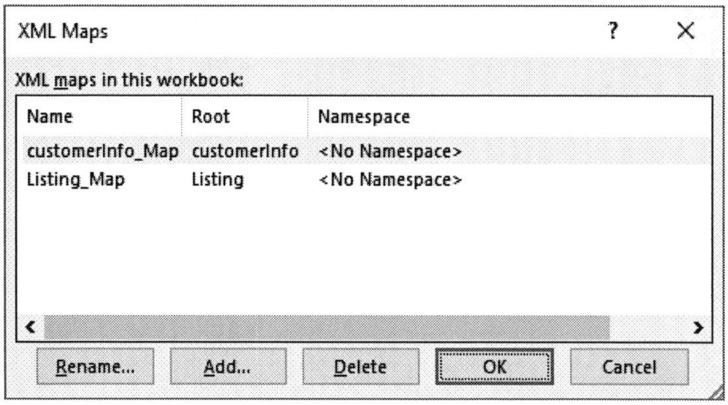

XML Maps		? ☓
XML maps in this workbook:		
Name	**Root**	**Namespace**
customerInfo_Map	customerInfo	<No Namespace>
Listing_Map	Listing	<No Namespace>

| Rename... | Add... | Delete | OK | Cancel |

Figure E-4: The XML Maps dialog box.

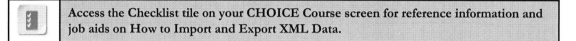
Access the Checklist tile on your CHOICE Course screen for reference information and job aids on How to Import and Export XML Data.

F | Internationalizing Workbooks

Appendix Introduction

In this appendix, you'll learn how to internationalize workbooks.

TOPIC A

Internationalize Workbooks

In today's globalized environment, competing in the international marketplace is critical. As such, you may find yourself exchanging information with colleagues and clients all over the world and analyzing data from users in multiple countries. While this can certainly be good for business, it can also present its fair share of challenges. Just a few simple examples can make this clear. People in different parts of the world use entirely different languages with unique sets of characters and symbols. Some languages are written from right to left instead of the left-to-right orientation western users are used to. And, particular font types work better for some languages than others. Fortunately, Microsoft® Office Excel® 2016 includes a set of functionality and options, in addition to the language and editing options, that enable you to present your data and analysis to users in other countries in formats they can more easily comprehend. Taking the time to understand how these options and functionality work can help you remain competitive in an increasingly globalized marketplace.

Worksheet and Worksheet Tab Direction

Excel users in some parts of the world are used to reading from right to left, quite the opposite of most western users. So, it may be helpful for your workbook recipients to receive your workbook files in a format they're used to reading. Excel 2016 provides you with the option to switch the direction of your overall workbook layout from the western default of left-to-right, to right-to-left. When you change this setting, the column headers appear in "reverse" alphabetical order beginning at the top-right corner of your worksheets, and the row headers appear vertically along the right side of worksheets. The worksheet tabs also appear on the right side of the screen and appear in numeric order, based on the default worksheet names, from right to left. Changing this setting also reverses the direction the **Tab** key navigates to accommodate the reverse layout.

While the overall layout of your worksheets changes when you switch this setting, it is your currently installed and selected language settings and options that affect the flow of text. If you retain English (US), for example, as your display language, even with the workbook layout reversed, your text will appear in the left-to-right orientation within worksheet cells. It is also important to realize that workbooks created in one layout retain that layout even when opened in an instance of Excel that is configured in the opposite layout.

 Note: For more information on changing the installed display and Help languages in Excel 2016, select the **How do I get more Display and Help languages from Office.com?** link in the **Choose Display and Help Languages** section of the **Language** tab in the **Excel Options** dialog box.

Switching the worksheet layout and tab direction is an application-level setting that requires you to close and restart Excel to take effect. You can access this option in the **Display** section on the **Advanced** tab of the **Excel Options** dialog box.

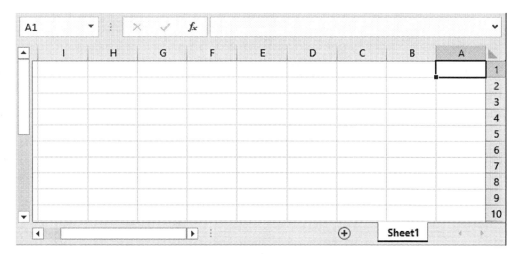

Figure F–1: An Excel worksheet in the right-to-left orientation.

The Symbol Dialog Box

If you need to insert characters specific to some international language or particular discipline, use the **Symbol** dialog box. From here you can select the font set and subset for which you need to include a symbol, select the desired symbol, and then insert it into your worksheets. You can also use the **Symbol** dialog box to insert special characters—such as copyright and trademark signs, and en and em dashes. You can access the **Symbol** dialog box by selecting **Insert→Symbols→Symbol**.

Figure F–2: The Symbols tab of the Symbol dialog box.

International Number Formatting

It stands to reason that, as you interact with other users in various parts of the world, you're going to need access to formatting options for your worksheet data that match the format those users are used to seeing. Simple examples include the way dates and times are expressed, how ZIP codes are formatted, and how international phone number formats vary. Monetary values also often have different symbols to represent them depending on where you are in the world. So, Excel 2016 provides you with some additional formatting options for some of the categories of number formatting in the **Format Cells** dialog box.

Two of the categories for which there are additional, international formatting options are the **Currency** and the **Accounting** categories. When you select either of these categories, the **Format Cells** dialog box displays the **Symbol** drop-down menu. From there, you can select the appropriate currency symbol for your needs, which changes the formatting options available for you to apply to worksheet cells. In the **Date**, **Time**, and **Special** categories, the **Format Cells** dialog box displays the **Locale (location)** drop-down menu. From there, you can select the appropriate country or region for your purposes, which, again, displays a number of different options for formatting your cells.

Format Cells	?	X

Number | Alignment | Font | Border | Fill | Protection

Category:

General
Number
Currency
Accounting
Date
Time
Percentage
Fraction
Scientific
Text
Special
Custom

Sample

Type:

*3/14/2012
*Wednesday, March 14, 2012
3/14
3/14/12
03/14/12
14-Mar
14-Mar-12

Locale (location):

English (United States)

Spanish (Argentina)
Spanish (Bolivia)
Spanish (Chile)
Spanish (Colombia)
Spanish (Costa Rica)
Spanish (Cuba)

Date formats display date and time serial numbers as date values. Date formats that begin with an asterisk (*) respond to changes in regional date and time settings that are specified for the operating system. Formats without an asterisk are not affected by operating system settings.

OK | Cancel

Figure F–3: Selecting various options from the Symbol and Locale (location) drop-down menus provides you with additional, international number formatting options.

Heading and Body Fonts

When you select editing language and keyboard layout options in Excel 2016, by default, the application's heading and body fonts are changed to match. If your language preference is English (US), your default heading and body font is Calibri. But, other languages may use different fonts, and a language's default font could be different for body text versus heading text. By default, your current language's body font is the default text font for data in worksheet cells. But, you can change this from the **General** tab in the **Excel Options** dialog box if you'd like. Body and heading font settings also determine the text font for items like text, titles, and labels in graphical objects such as shapes and charts.

 Access the Checklist tile on your CHOICE Course screen for reference information and job aids on How to Internationalize a Workbook.

G | Working with Power Pivot

Appendix Introduction

In this appendix, you'll learn how to work with Power Pivot.

TOPIC A

Work with Power Pivot

You are already aware of Excel's many analytical capabilities. And, for as powerful as Microsoft® Office Excel® 2016 is, there are some tasks it simply can't handle on its own. There may be times in your career where you need to perform complex data analysis on very large datasets from a wide variety of sources, which may include data in numerous database tables or from massive data feeds. When your analysis requires this sort of heavy lifting, Excel could use a bit of help. Fortunately, Excel 2016 includes a powerful add-in that can handle this very type of heavy lifting: Power Pivot. Taking the time to become familiar with this add-in, its capabilities, and how it works will open an array of new opportunities in terms of high-level data analysis.

 Note: As Power Pivot is a robust tool with powerful capabilities, a complete examination of its functionality is well beyond the scope of this course. While the information here is meant to provide you with a solid introduction to Power Pivot and its capabilities, Logical Operations recommends you attend a formal Power Pivot training event to achieve a high level of proficiency with this tool.

Power Pivot

Power Pivot is an Excel add-in that provides users with additional data analysis and modeling capabilities. It comes bundled with Excel 2016, but it is disabled by default. While Excel contains native functionality for importing data from various sources and analyzing that data using PivotTables, the Power Pivot add-in takes that functionality to a higher level. For example, Power Pivot enables you to filter data and rename fields while importing data, view tables and table relationships in both tabular and graphical views, manage relationships among tables in your dataset, and write advanced formulas to analyze complex datasets.

Data that you manage and analyze using Excel and the Power Pivot add-in is stored in a database within your Excel workbook files. This analytical database uses a built-in engine to provide the functionality for querying and managing your data. Data stored in this database is available to both Excel and Power Pivot simultaneously, so you can analyze the data using any of Excel's native functionality, like PivotTables and other add-ins that provide even greater modeling and presentation functionality.

The Power Pivot Tab

When you activate the Power Pivot add-in, Excel displays the **Power Pivot** tab. You will use the commands and options here to open Power Pivot, manage your dataset and table relationships, and configure Power Pivot options and settings.

Figure G-1: The Power Pivot tab.

The following table describes the types of commands you will find in the various groups on the **Power Pivot** tab.

Power Pivot Tab Group	Contains Commands For
Data Model	Opening Power Pivot or navigating to the Power Pivot window from Excel when Power Pivot is open.
Calculations	Creating and managing calculated fields and key performance indicators (KPIs).
Tables	Adding tables to the data model and updating table data.
Relationships	Managing relationships among tables in the data model.

The **Power Pivot** tab also displays an unnamed group that contains the **Settings** command. This command opens the **Power Pivot Settings** dialog box, which provides you with access to support and diagnostic resources and Power Pivot application settings.

The Data Model

Analyzing data from a variety of different sources using Excel and Power Pivot is dependent on the *Data Model*. The Data Model consists of the relationships among the various tables contained in a particular workbook. Two or more tables can be related to each other if they contain a common field (column) between or among them and the columns contain unique entries. Once the relationship is established, Excel and Power Pivot can make sense of how the data in the various tables relate to each other.

For example, suppose you need to analyze data about your customers and their purchasing behavior. But, also suppose that customer information is stored in one table and purchasing information is stored in another table. If you'd like to determine which customers, based on their regional locations, purchase more of a certain product than others, you'll need a way for Excel and Power Pivot to "know" something about customer locations and their purchases. If there is a common column in both of those tables, say a CustomerID column, and you establish a relationship between the two tables based on that common column, Excel and Power Pivot can look down the entries in the customer information table, look up a particular customer's location, then look for that common customer ID in the purchases table, and then look up what the customer purchased. Essentially, it's the same as both location and purchasing entries being entered in the same row of a single larger table that contains all of the information. Establishing relationships among tables means that Excel and Power Pivot can match the data from the various tables based on a common set of entries among them.

When you import data using Power Pivot, and that data is stored in tables with existing relationships, Power Pivot maintains those relationships automatically. You can, however, also manually create relationships among unrelated datasets and manage your existing relationships. It is this data-modeling functionality that makes Power Pivot such a powerful analytical add-in.

The Power Pivot User Interface

The Power Pivot user interface (UI) contains a variety of commands and workspaces you will use to manage your Data Models and analyze your data. Remember, the information in your Data Models is available to both Excel and Power Pivot, so you can also use any of Excel's native functionality to analyze and present all of the data in your Data Models. The Power Pivot UI is divided into two main components: the ribbon and a workspace pane.

The workspace pane can either display the tables in your Data Models in tabular form or in a graphical form that enables you to view and manage table relationships. The ribbon contains the tabs and command groups that provide you with access to the commands you need to work with your data, similar to Excel's ribbon.

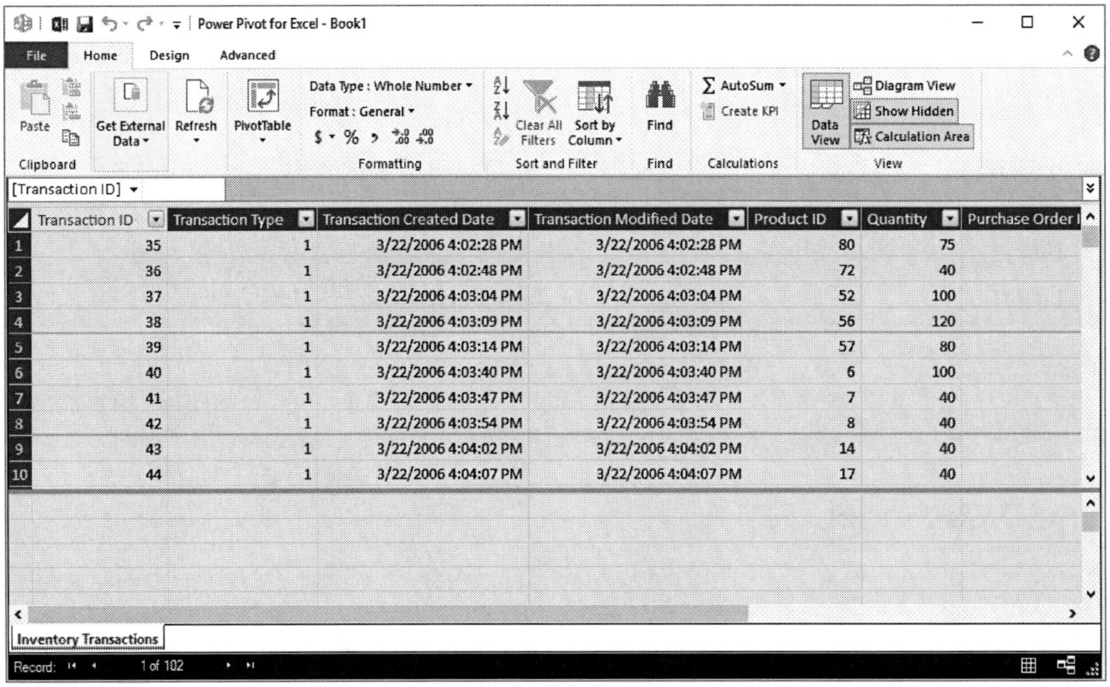

Figure G-2: The Power Pivot UI in the Data view.

The following table describes the types of commands you will find within the various command groups on the Power Pivot UI ribbon.

Power Pivot Ribbon Tab	Contains Commands For
File	Managing your Power Pivot and Excel files.
Home	Copying and pasting data; importing, formatting, and updating data; creating PivotTables and PivotCharts from the Data Model; searching for data; performing advanced calculations on your data; and managing your Power Pivot views.
Design	Managing table layouts, inserting functions and calculations, managing Data Model relationships, and configuring table properties.
Advanced	Creating and managing views of data subsets, aggregating numeric column data, and setting properties for external reporting tools.

The Data and Diagram Views

There are two main ways for you to view your Data Model within the Power Pivot UI: the **Data** view and the **Diagram** view. In the **Data** view, Power Pivot displays the tables in your Data Models on a series of tabs in tabular form. In other words, the **Data** view enables you to view all of your Data Model tables, their columns, and their entries individually and completely.

The **Diagram** view displays the relationships among the tables in your Data Models in graphical form. From here, you can also use GUI-based functionality to manage relationships among the tables in your Data Models. You can switch between these two views using the commands in the **View** group on the Power Pivot ribbon's **Home** tab.

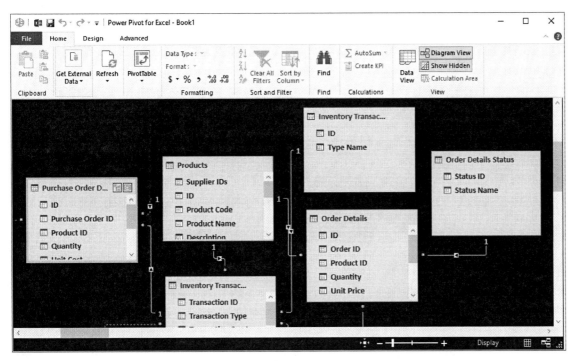

Figure G-3: The Power Pivot UI in the Diagram view.

The Create Relationship Dialog Box

In addition to being able to graphically create and manage relationships among tables in the Data Model while in the **Diagram** view, you can also create and manage relationships using the **Create Relationship** dialog box. Remember, in order to create relationships among or between tables, the tables must all contain a common field (column), and those columns must contain unique entries. You can access the **Create Relationship** dialog box by selecting **Design→Relationships→Create Relationship** on the Power Pivot ribbon.

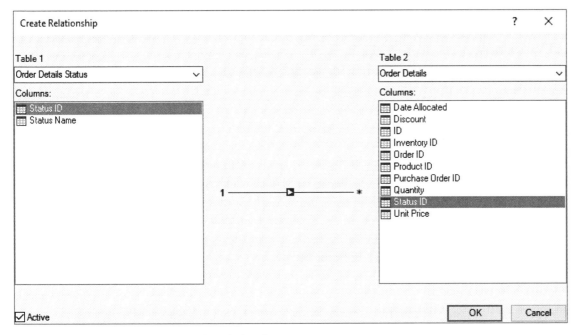

Figure G-4: The Create Relationship dialog box.

The following table describes the various elements of the **Create Relationship** dialog box.

Create Relationship Dialog Box Element	Use This To
Table 1 and **Table 2** drop-down menu	Select the tables you wish to relate to one another.
Columns list box	Select the column from which you wish to establish the relationship for each table.
Active check box	Make the relationship between the two tables active or inactive. An inactive relationship appears as a dotted line.
OK button	Establish the configured relationship.
Cancel button	Cancel the process of creating a relationship and close the **Create Relationship** dialog box.

Calculated Columns

One of the truly powerful features of Power Pivot is its ability to aggregate values based on existing table entries that you can then use to populate PivotTable reports. To generate these aggregate values, you can add *calculated columns* to your tables. You can then drag these calculated columns to the various areas in the **PivotTable Fields** task pane to populate your PivotTables as you would with any other field in a dataset.

In Power Pivot, you create calculated columns by creating a new, empty column within a table, and then entering a specialized formula, known as a Data Analysis Expression (DAX) formula, in the column's cells that calculates or returns the desired aggregate information in each row based on entries in other related table columns. Selecting the entire column simultaneously enters the DAX formula into all cells in a column in much the same way as you add array formulas to ranges in Excel worksheets. In fact, you cannot enter different DAX formulas in the various rows of the same column; you can only apply a single formula to the entire column at once.

> **Note:** A complete examination of DAX formulas and their syntax is beyond the scope of this topic. For more information on DAX formulas, please visit **office.microsoft.com**.

By default, Power Pivot adds calculated columns to the right of the existing columns in a table and assigns them default names, such as *CalculatedColumn1*. You can, however, arrange and rename calculated columns as needed, as long as you follow a few guidelines:

- All column names, including calculated columns, should be unique within a given table.
- If your Data Model contains calculated fields, while it is possible to duplicate the names, it's recommended you do not name a calculated column the same name as a calculated field.
- Values in a calculated column must be updated before you can rename the column.
- Power Pivot does not support spaces and certain characters in calculated column names, but you may be able to circumvent this by enclosing the name in double quotation marks (" ").

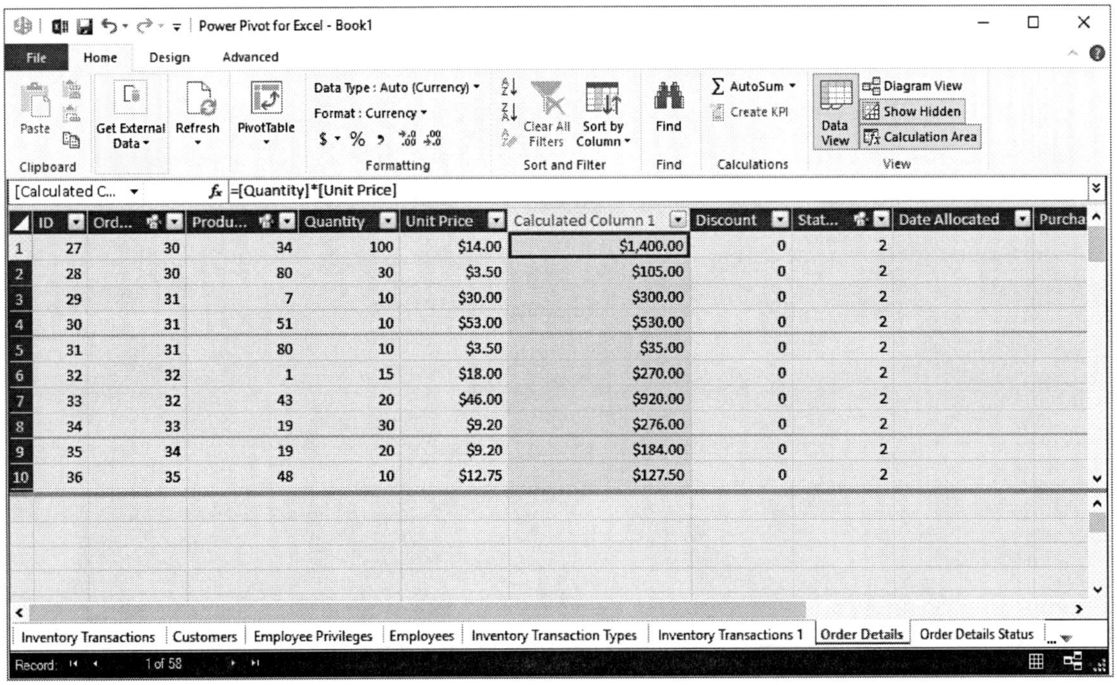

ID	Ord...	Produ...	Quantity	Unit Price	Calculated Column 1	Discount	Stat...	Date Allocated	Purcha
27	30	34	100	$14.00	$1,400.00	0	2		
28	30	80	30	$3.50	$105.00	0	2		
29	31	7	10	$30.00	$300.00	0	2		
30	31	51	10	$53.00	$530.00	0	2		
31	31	80	10	$3.50	$35.00	0	2		
32	32	1	15	$18.00	$270.00	0	2		
33	32	43	20	$46.00	$920.00	0	2		
34	33	19	30	$9.20	$276.00	0	2		
35	34	19	20	$9.20	$184.00	0	2		
36	35	48	10	$12.75	$127.50	0	2		

Figure G-5: A calculated column in a Data Model table with its DAX formula displayed in the Formula Bar.

Access the Checklist tile on your CHOICE Course screen for reference information and job aids on How to Work with Power Pivot.

H | Advanced Customization Options

Appendix Introduction

In this appendix, you'll learn how to customize advanced options.

TOPIC A

Customize Advanced Options

Microsoft® Office Excel® 2016 provides you with a vast array of options for changing the behind the scenes behavior of the application to suit organizational or specific user needs. Knowing where to find these options, and what each of them does, will make it easy for your to quickly adjust Excel's default behavior whenever the need arises.

Formulas Options

The **Formulas** tab in the **Excel Options** dialog box contains settings that affect how Excel works with and displays formulas and functions, and how error-checking features behave.

Formulas Tab Section	Contains Options For
Calculation options	Configuring how Excel executes calculations in functions and formulas.
Working with formulas	Toggling formula features on or off.
Error Checking	Toggling automatic error checking on or off, and changing the display of discovered errors.
Error checking rules	Toggling particular error-checking rules on or off.

Proofing Options

The **Proofing** tab in the **Excel Options** dialog box contains settings that affect how Excel performs AutoCorrect and spelling check functions.

Proofing Tab Section	Description
AutoCorrect options	Displays the **AutoCorrect Options** button, which opens the **AutoCorrect** dialog box.
When correcting spelling in Microsoft Office programs	Contains options for managing how Excel and other Office applications check for misspellings, for selecting the dictionary against which Excel checks word spellings, and for configuring particular language-specific options.

The AutoCorrect Dialog Box

The **AutoCorrect** dialog box contains settings for managing how Excel automatically corrects spelling and other data entry issues as you type. It is divided into a series of four tabs that contain related settings options.

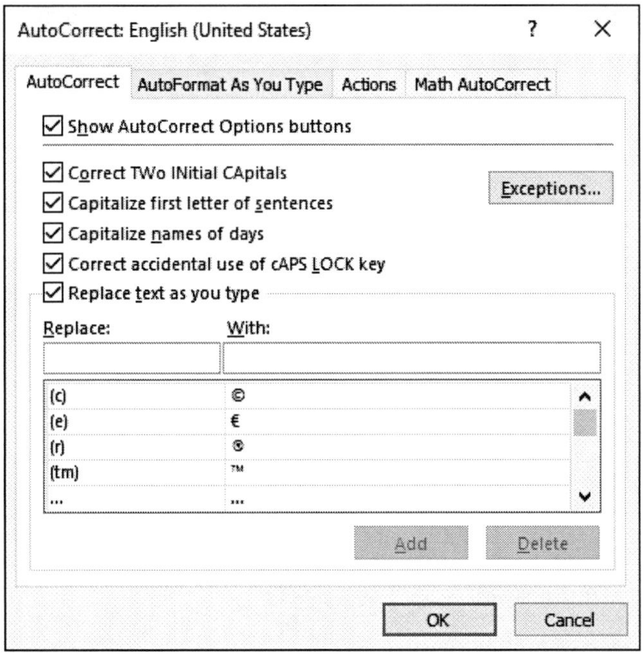

Figure H-1: Use the AutoCorrect dialog box to configure how Excel corrects common misspellings.

AutoCorrect Dialog Box Tab	Contains Options For
AutoCorrect	Toggling specific AutoCorrect functionality on and off, such as whether or not Excel automatically capitalizes the first word of a sentence if you forget to. From here, you can also manage how Excel automatically corrects common typing errors such as replacing "teh" with "the."
AutoFormat As You Type	Toggling particular AutoFormatting options on or off, such as whether or not Excel automatically formats URLs as hyperlinks.
Actions	Enabling or disabling additional automatic actions in context menus.
Math AutoCorrect	Managing how Excel automatically enters mathematical symbols in the Equation Editor based on keyboard input. For example, by default, if you type \pi, Excel replaces the text with the mathematical symbol π.

Save Options

The **Save** tab in the **Excel Options** dialog box contains settings that affect how and to which directory Excel saves workbook files.

Save Tab Section	Contains Options For
Save workbooks	Selecting the default file format that Excel saves workbooks in, for determining how often Excel automatically saves unsaved workbooks, and for selecting the default directories for saving workbooks and for the AutoRecover feature.
AutoRecover Exceptions for	Enabling or disabling the AutoRecover feature for particular workbooks.

Save Tab Section	Contains Options For
Offline editing options for document management server files	Selecting where Excel saves draft copies of workbook files that you check out of a Microsoft® SharePoint® site.
Preserve visual appearance of the workbook	Selecting or modifying the color palette that Excel will use when opening a workbook in a previous version of Excel.

Language Options

The **Language** tab in the **Excel Options** dialog box contains settings that affect which languages and dictionaries Excel references for a variety of purposes.

Language Tab Section	Contains Options For
Choose Editing Languages	Adding or removing languages Excel will use to check for spelling, grammar, and other language-related issues.
Choose Display and Help Languages	Selecting which language to use for the display of command and tab names, and within the Excel Help system.

Note: For more information on customizing Excel's language options, access the LearnTO **Add Languages to Microsoft Excel** presentation from the **LearnTO** tile on the CHOICE course screen.

Advanced Options

The **Advanced** tab in the **Excel Options** dialog box contains settings that affect a wide array of commonly used Excel functionality. The options on the **Advanced** tab will likely have the greatest overall effect on your Excel user experience. The following table identifies the types of option settings you will find in some of the more commonly used sections of the **Advanced** tab.

Advanced Tab Section	Contains Options For
Editing options	Configuring navigation functionality, configuring data entry and editing settings, and toggling features such as AutoFill and AutoComplete on or off.
Cut, copy, and paste	Toggling various cut, copy, and paste functionality on or off.
Image Size and Quality	Determining whether or not Excel compresses graphical objects saved in workbooks, and for setting the default graphics resolution level.
Print	Enabling or disabling high quality mode, which determines the overall print quality of objects in worksheets.
Chart	Toggling the display of particular chart elements on or off.
Display	Managing the overall display of the Excel application window. From here, you can set the number of recent documents that are displayed in the **Backstage** view, set the default unit of measurement for rulers, and toggle on or off the display of screen elements such as the **Formula Bar** and comment indicators.
Display options for this workbook	Managing the display of particular workbooks. From here, you can toggle the display of user interface (UI) elements such as scroll bars and worksheet tabs on or off.

Advanced Tab Section	Contains Options For
Display options for this worksheet	Managing the display of particular worksheets. From here, you can toggle the view of column and row headers on or off, decide whether to display formulas or values in cells, toggle the view of gridlines on or off, and change the color of worksheet gridlines.
Formulas	Adjust how much computing power is used to calculate formulas.
When calculating this workbook	Managing how Excel deals with links to other documents and how the display of numeric values affects the accuracy of calculations.
General	Managing a wide array of application-wide settings, such as whether or not sounds play when you make a mistake, and whether or not Excel prompts you to update links to external documents.
Data	Options for managing large amounts of data in PivotTables or with Power Pivot.
Lotus compatibility	Provides shortcut keys to enable Lotus 1-2-3 methods of navigation in Excel.
Lotus compatibility Settings for	Enables options for working with Lotus 1-2-3 files in Excel.

 Note: You can also switch between displaying results in cells and displaying formulas in cells for the currently selected worksheet by pressing **Ctrl+~**.

Custom Lists

One handy feature that can save you time when developing workbooks is custom lists. These lists work with the AutoFill feature to make entering repetitive data entries fast and easy. Once you create a custom list, you can begin entering the list items in a series of contiguous cells and then use the AutoFill feature to complete the process of entering the list by using the **fill handle**. This can come in handy when you need to enter the same information, say an employee list or the steps in an organizational process, into worksheets on a regular basis.

You create custom lists using the **Custom Lists** dialog box, which you can access in the **General** section of the **Advanced** tab in the **Excel Options** dialog box. You can either manually type new custom lists or create them from existing cell entries. You can also edit or delete custom lists. By default, Excel 2016 comes loaded with four included custom lists: the long and the abbreviated forms of the days of the week and the months of the year. You cannot modify or delete these default custom lists.

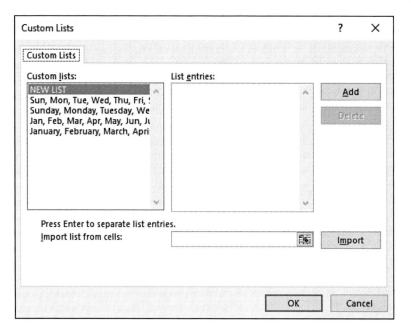

Figure H-2: Use the Custom Lists dialog box to create and manage custom lists.

Add-Ins

Add-ins are supplemental programs for Microsoft Office applications that provide additional features and functionality not available in a standard installation. Some add-ins, such as the Analysis ToolPak and the Solver add-in, come installed with Excel and are simply inactive by default. You can download other add-ins from Microsoft, or a host of other sources, and then activate them. You can also develop custom add-ins to enhance Excel's functionality, if you have the programming acumen to do so. Add-ins must be enabled for you to have access to their features and functionality.

The Add-Ins Tab

You can view and manage your Excel add-ins on the **Add-Ins** tab in the **Excel Options** dialog box. From here, you can view all add-ins that are installed on your computer, and all add-ins that are both installed and enabled. This is also where you can access dialog boxes for the various add-in types, which allow you to enable and disable add-ins as needed.

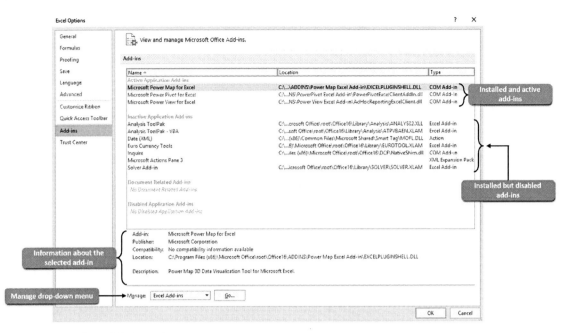

Figure H-3: The Add-Ins tab.

The following table describes some of the key elements of the **Add-Ins** tab.

Add-Ins Tab Element	Enables You To
Active Application Add-ins section	View a list of all add-ins currently installed and enabled on your computer.
Inactive Application Add-ins section	View a list of all add-ins that are currently installed on your computer but that are disabled.
Type column	View add-in types. These typically give you a clue to the general functionality or features the add-in provides for Excel.
Add-in information	View additional information about the currently selected add-in.
Manage drop-down menu	Access the dialog boxes for the various add-in types. From these dialog boxes, you can enable or disable add-ins as needed.

The Trust Center

The **Trust Center** tab provides you with access to information about Excel privacy and security policies along with commands for changing privacy and security settings. From here, you can follow a number of links to published security and privacy policies or open the **Trust Center** dialog box, which is where you can configure privacy and security settings. You can access the **Trust Center** dialog box by selecting the **Trust Center Settings** button.

> **Note:** Microsoft recommends consulting with your system administrator before changing **Trust Center** settings, as these may greatly increase or decrease your computer and network security.

The Trust Center Dialog Box

The **Trust Center** dialog box is divided into 12 tabs that provide you with access to groups of related security and privacy options.

Trust Center Tab	Allows You To
Trusted Publishers	Generate a list of publishers you trust. Outside content from trusted publishers is not subject to the same validation process as content from non-trusted publishers.
Trusted Locations	Specify folders on your computer in which you would like to store trusted files. Content from these folders is not subject to the same security and validation process as content from other folders.
Trusted Documents	Manage how Excel treats trusted documents. Once you've trusted a document, Excel no longer subjects it to the same security validation process. You should trust documents only if you truly trust the source of the documents.
Trusted Add-in Catalogs	Enable or disable Office apps in Excel and specify which web add-in catalogs you trust.
Add-ins	Enable or disable the use of Excel add-ins and specify whether or not add-ins require security certificates.
ActiveX Settings	Manage how Excel interacts with files containing active content. Active content can contain malicious code.
Macro Settings	Enable or disable the use of macros and manage how Excel interacts with workbook files containing macros.
Protected View	Specify whether or not files from particular sources, such as the Internet or email attachments, will cause Excel to open them in Protected view.
Message Bar	Specify whether or not Excel displays a warning whenever files containing active content are opened.
External Content	Manage security settings for dealing with external data sources and workbooks.
File Block Settings	Specify which file formats prompt Excel to open in Protected view.
Privacy Options	Toggle various privacy settings on or off and access the **Document Inspector**, which allows you to remove personal information, such as the author's name, from files before you share them with other users.

 Note: For a more in-depth examination of the Trust Center, access the LearnTO **Ensure the Security of Your Excel Environment** presentation from the **LearnTO** tile on the CHOICE course screen.

 Access the Checklist tile on your CHOICE Course screen for reference information and job aids on How to Configure Excel Options.

Access the Checklist tile on your CHOICE Course screen for reference information and job aids on How to Enable Add-Ins.

Working with Forms and Controls

Appendix Introduction

In this appendix, you'll work with forms and controls.

TOPIC A

Work with Forms and Controls

Although data entry in Excel worksheets is typically fairly straightforward, some worksheets require excessive scrolling for users to be able to access all cells. Other worksheets may require users to enter data that is difficult to type, such as technical jargon or complex numeric figures. Whatever the reason, you may find yourself in charge of a workbook that some users find difficult to work with. So, it would be helpful if you could include or take advantage of functionality to help those users complete the task at hand.

Fortunately, Microsoft® Office Excel® 2016 provides you with a number of options for helping users enter data. Whether for saving them the time and effort it takes to navigate around large worksheets or for providing quick and easy access to the data they need to supply, your workbook users will thank you for taking the time to include this additional functionality. And you'll enjoy the benefits of managing workbooks that aren't full of errors and getting the data you need from your colleagues quickly.

Forms

Making it easy for users to add data to Excel worksheets typically involves working with some type of *form*. A form is either a physical or an electronic document that is organized for the purpose of collecting information. You are likely familiar with all manner of forms, such as those you might fill out at a doctor's office, when applying for a job, or when ordering items from a catalog. An electronic form is much the same as a physical form, except it exists as an electronic document, not on paper, and may contain additional functionality, such as buttons and interactive menus, that can help you fill in the required information.

Although Excel spreadsheets are often used for storing and analyzing organizational data, they contain a fair amount of built-in functionality that also makes them suitable for creating electronic forms. For example, you can create forms that new hires might use to enter their personal and employee information. Because they would be entering that information directly into Excel, you could then take advantage of Excel's organizational and analytical capabilities to work with the information without first having to perform data entry. You can use these same capabilities to simply make entering data easier for other, more typical, workbook uses.

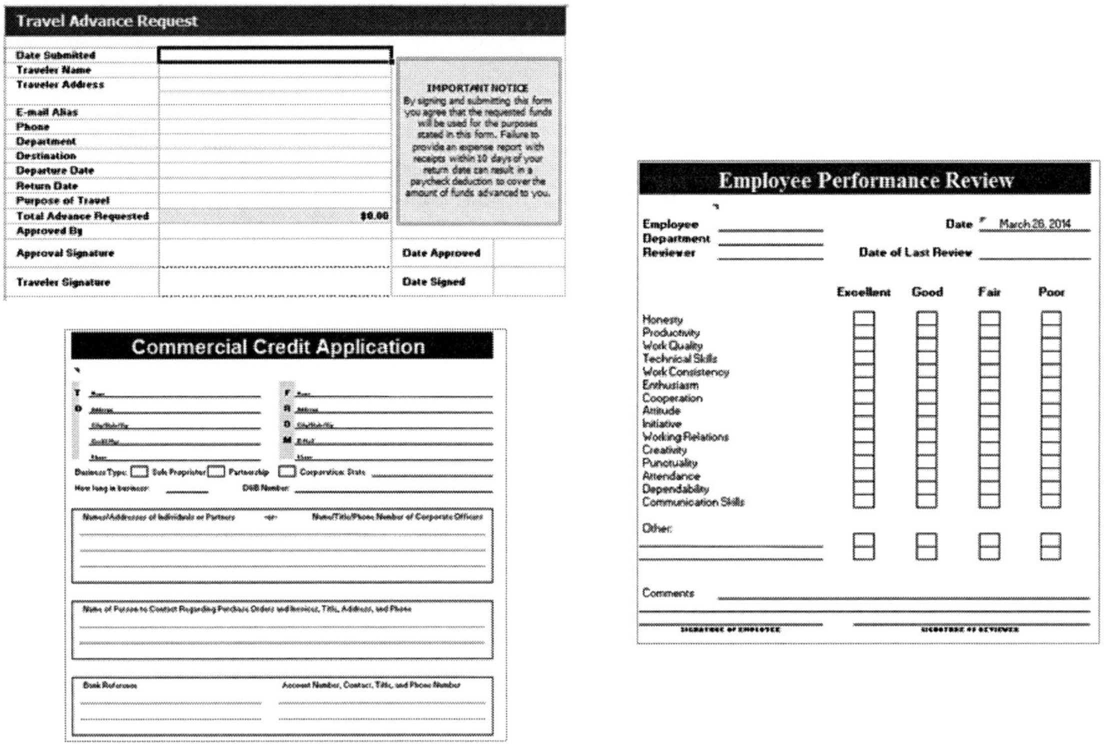

Figure I-1: A sampling of Excel forms.

Form Types

There are three basic types of forms you can create using Excel: data forms, worksheets that contain form controls, and VBA UserForms. Each of the form types contains varying degrees of functionality and would typically be used for particular purposes.

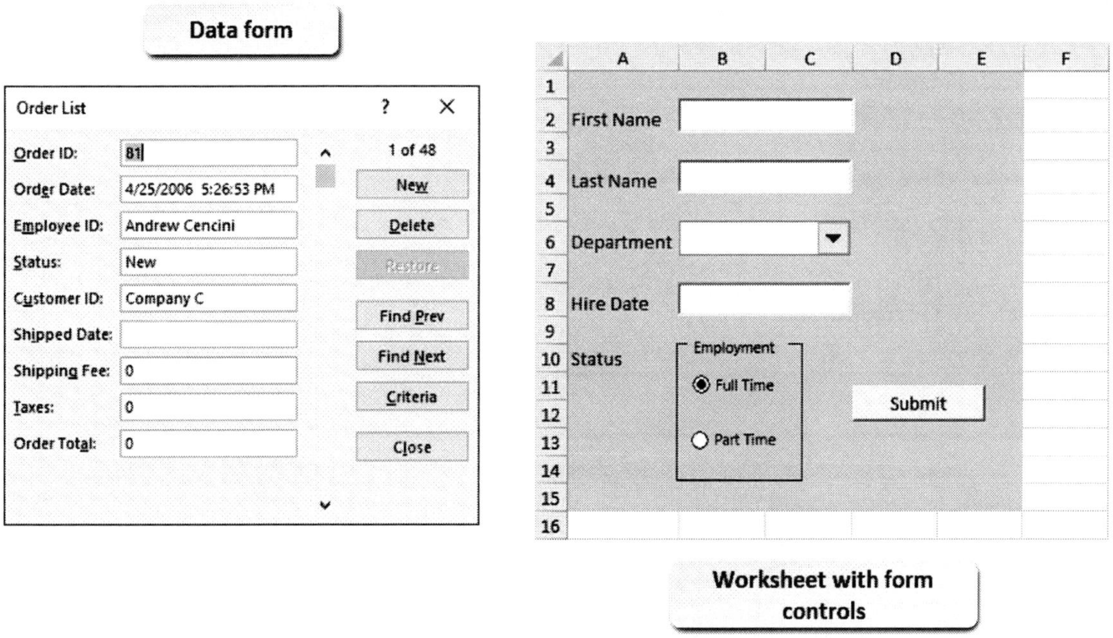

Figure I-2: A data form and a worksheet that contains form controls.

The following table provides a brief description of the types of Excel forms.

Form Type	Description
Data forms	A data form makes entering data into worksheets that contain a large number of columns quick and easy. Excel automatically creates these forms for you based on the column labels in your dataset. The main advantage of using data forms is the fact that you don't have to scroll horizontally to enter data all the way at the end of long rows. But data forms also allow users to easily search for a particular entry (row) of data, view all column headers in a single window, and take advantage of simple tabbed navigation. You must add the **Form** control to the **Quick Access Toolbar** or the ribbon to generate data forms.
Worksheets with form controls	Worksheets made into forms closely resemble the physical paper forms you have likely filled out on many occasions. They are predominantly used to gather information. Text labels on worksheet forms inform users of what information to include in which cells. Additionally, you can include form controls that make it easier for the user to add particular information.
VBA UserForms	VBA UserForms are highly customized dialog boxes that can be used to enter information or data on worksheets. However, UserForms are not limited to this task. You can create UserForms to help you perform a wide variety of tasks, and they can be used in any Office application that supports apps created in Microsoft's Visual Basic® for Applications (VBA) programming language. In Excel 2016, and other Office applications, you create and program VBA UserForms in the Visual Basic Editor.

The Developer Tab

In order to create forms and develop other types of additional capabilities in Excel 2016, you must first display the **Developer** ribbon tab. The *Developer tab* is included with Excel 2016, but by default, it is inactive. The **Developer** tab is divided into four groups that provide you with access to the tools and commands you can use to custom develop additional Excel functionality.

Figure I-3: Add the Developer tab to the ribbon to access additional Excel capabilities.

The following table identifies the types of commands you will find within the various command groups on the **Developer** tab.

Developer Tab Command Group	Contains Commands For
Code	Developing and managing macros and creating applications using the Visual Basic Editor.
Add-Ins	Managing Excel add-ins. This group contains shortcuts to the **Add-Ins** dialog box and the **COM Add-Ins** dialog box, which you can also access in the **Excel Options** dialog box.
Controls	Working with forms and controls.

Developer Tab Command Group	Contains Commands For
XML	Accessing XML coding capabilities, developing XML code, and importing or exporting XML files.

Form Controls

Controls are objects you can add to your worksheets that help users perform certain tasks, such as entering data or making a selection in a cell linked to the control. In Excel, there are two types of controls: *form controls* and *ActiveX controls*. Form controls provide you with an easy way to add functionality to your worksheets without having to use VBA code. Form controls are compatible with earlier versions of Excel, dating back to Excel 5.0, but cannot be used on VBA UserForms. In addition to helping users make selections or enter content into worksheets, you can configure form controls to run either existing or new macros. To access the form controls you can add to your worksheets, select **Developer→Controls→Insert**.

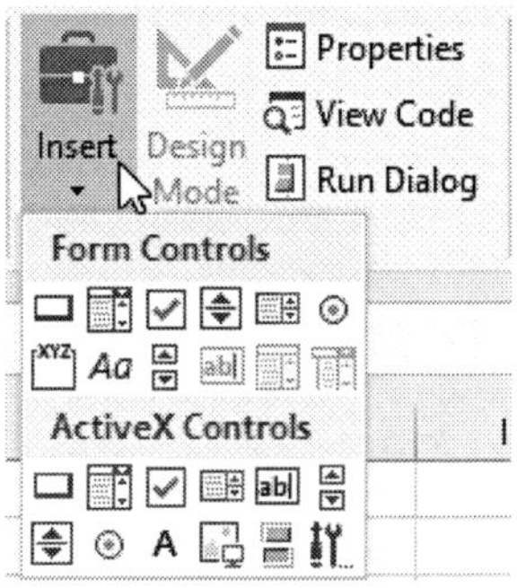

Figure I-4: Form controls add functionality to Excel worksheets.

The following table describes the function of the nine form controls supported by Excel 2016.

> **Note:** Several other form controls appear in the **Insert** drop-down menu in the **Controls** group on the **Developer** tab, but they are inactive as Excel 2016 does not support them.

Form Control	Icon Image	Function
Button	▭	These form controls are also known as "push buttons." You can configure these to run macros.
Combo Box	▤	Combo boxes combine a drop-down list box with a text box that displays the item a user selects from the list. The list box part of a combo box is similar to the standard list box form control. But with combo boxes, the list box is minimized until the user selects the drop-down arrow. Combo boxes return the index value, an entry's numeric place in the list, of the selected item in the linked cell, so you can use them in combination with the INDEX function to return the selected item in any cell other than the linked cell, or in combination with Lookup functions to return entries from datasets.

Form Control	Icon Image	Function
Check Box	☑	Check boxes typically return a logical value of either TRUE or FALSE in the linked cell. This means you can use them in combination with logical functions to add functionality to your worksheets. A checked check box returns the value TRUE, whereas an unchecked check box returns the value FALSE. There is a third possible state for check boxes: mixed. A check box in the mixed state appears shaded and returns a value of #N/A. An example of a check box that might appear in this state is a "select all" check box for a group of other check boxes. If some of those check boxes are checked and some not, the "select all" check box will be in the mixed state. Users can check more than one check box at a time on a worksheet or within a group box.
Spin Button	⬍	Spin boxes allow users to increase or decrease the value in the linked cell by a specified increment. You can set the minimum and maximum values, and the incremental value to suit your needs. Users are also typically able to manually enter values in the linked cell. Because spin buttons return numeric values, you can use the returned value in most formulas and functions.
List Box	▦	List boxes return the index value of the selected item in the linked cell. Unlike combo boxes, list boxes always appear full size, so they can take up a lot of space. Use list boxes in combination with the INDEX function to return the selected item in any cell other than the linked cell, or in combination with Lookup functions to return entries from datasets.
Option Button	◉	These form controls are commonly referred to as radio buttons. Unlike check boxes, users can select only one radio button within the same worksheet or group box at a time. Radio buttons that are not grouped together in a group box will all be considered as part of the same selection. Radio buttons in a group box represent a single collection of radio buttons, meaning they represent a single decision point. For each collection of radio buttons, the selected radio button returns the index value of its place in the collection in the linked cell. So, like with other form controls, you can use the INDEX function, or other Lookup functions, in conjunction with option buttons.
Group Box	⌐xyz	Group boxes provide no real functionality on their own. You use group boxes to separate individual entries (a single bit of information) on a worksheet form. Typically, you would group check boxes or radio buttons for a particular selection within a group box. Group boxes segregate the controls they contain from other controls. So, for example, radio buttons within a group only affect each other, which is important as only one of a collection of radio buttons can typically be selected at any one time. Optionally, group boxes can contain descriptive labels.
Label	Aa	Labels do not provide additional functionality on your worksheets. You will use labels to help users identify the purpose of the controls on your worksheets. You do not, however, have to use labels as you can also use formatted text entered into cells for the same purpose.

Form Control	Icon Image	Function
Scroll Bar	▲▼	Scroll bars function similarly to spin box form controls. Use these to return any value from a specified range, at a specified increment in the linked cell. You would use scroll bars when any of a very large number of values could be used and when calculating a precise value is not critical.

ActiveX Controls

ActiveX controls perform many of the same functions as form controls, but they are far more flexible and customizable, and they are capable of providing far more complex functionality than their form control counterparts. Like form controls, you can work with ActiveX controls directly on your worksheets without the need for VBA coding. But, unlike form controls, ActiveX controls can run on VBA applications and VBA UserForms.

Control Properties

Once you've added a control to a worksheet, you need to configure its properties. *Control properties* assign the specific functionality you desire to the control, configure the desired visual formatting options, assign the linked cell, and determine how the control interacts with the associated worksheet. You set control properties by using the **Format Control** dialog box, which you can access by selecting **Developer→Controls→Properties** when you have a control selected, or by right-clicking the desired control and then selecting **Format Control**.

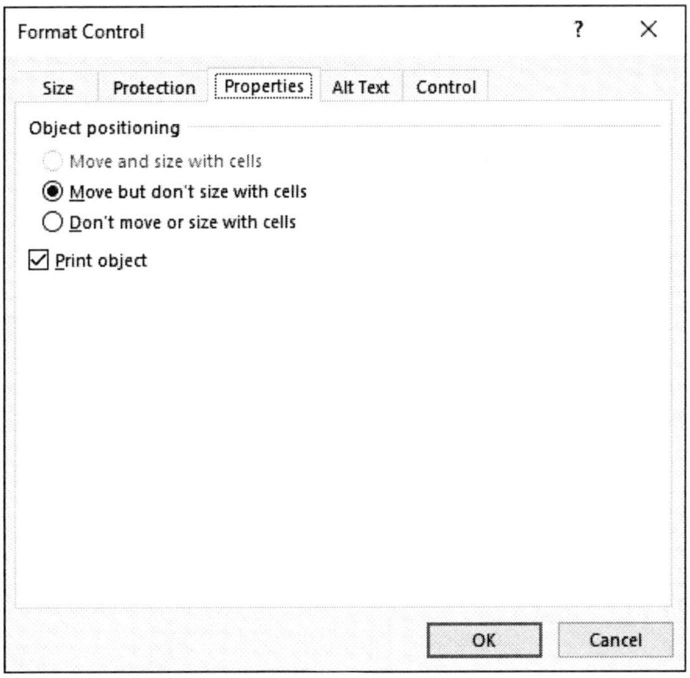

Figure I-5: The Format Control dialog box.

The following table outlines the properties you can set on the most common tabs in the **Format Control** dialog box.

 Note: Not all form controls will have all tabs in the **Format Control** dialog box. Additionally, you may encounter more tabs than are described here.

Format Control Dialog Box Tab	Contains Commands and Settings To
Size	Modify the size and orientation of the control.
Protection	Apply control protection to prevent users from making changes to your controls. As with cell protection formatting, these settings apply only if you protect the associated worksheet.
Properties	Determine how the control interacts with the cells on the associated worksheet. Although controls don't exist within cells, but rather on top of worksheets—in the way charts and other graphical objects do—you can configure them to change in size and location as you adjust column widths and row heights on the worksheet. On the **Properties** tab, you can also determine whether or not a control will appear on printed worksheets.
Alt Text	Include alternative text with worksheet controls. This can help users search for your worksheets if they are included on web pages, and can provide assistance to users with physical disabilities.
Control	Determine the linked cell, establish the default state of check boxes and radio buttons, set the input range for list boxes, and set the value parameters for spin buttons and scroll bars.

 Access the Checklist tile on your CHOICE Course screen for reference information and job aids on How to Work with Data Forms and Controls.

ACTIVITY I–1
Adding and Editing Data by Using a Data Form

Data File

C:\091057Data\Appendix I\My Author Master Roster.xlsx

Scenario

As other users will be adding and editing author information in the workbook, you have decided to add the **Form** command to the **Quick Access Toolbar**. Users can then manage the author roster easily and with fewer errors. As you have the workbook open, you also decide to correct some data you've discovered is incorrect, and to begin adding the information for a new author to the roster.

The data that you need to correct is for author 1032. These are the erroneous entries:

- Status: Active
- Genre: SciFi
- Payment Method: Ck

---

1. Add the **Form** command to the **Quick Access Toolbar**.

   a) On the **Quick Access Toolbar**, select the **Customize Quick Access Toolbar** button and then select **More Commands**.

   b) In the **Excel Options** dialog box, ensure that the **Quick Access Toolbar** tab is selected.

   c) From the **Choose commands from** drop-down menu, select **Commands Not in the Ribbon**.

   d) In the **Choose commands from** list, scroll down and select **Form**.

   e) Select **Add**, and then select **OK**.

2. Create a data form from the dataset on the **Authors** worksheet.

   a) From the **Authors** worksheet, select any cell within the dataset.

   b) On the **Quick Access Toolbar**, select the **Form** command.

3. Locate and correct an entry using the data form.

   a) In the **Authors** data form, select the **Criteria** button.

   b) In the **AuthorID** field, type *1032* and press **Enter**.

   c) Press **Tab** until the **Status** field is active and then type *Retained*

   d) Press **Tab** until the **Genre** field is active and then type *Romance*

e) Press **Tab** until the **Payment Method** field is active, type *DD* and press **Tab**.

Authors		? ✕
AuthorID:	1032	︿ 12 of 837
InitialContract Date:	1/6/2007	New
YearsUnder Contract:	7.05479452054795	Delete
Status:	Retained	Restore
Origin:	Legacy	
Genre:	Romance	Find Prev
Agent Code:	5072	Find Next
Payment Method:	DD	Criteria
State (if US):	NJ	Close
Country Code:	1	
Number of Titles in Print:	25	
Number ofBooks Sold:	595341	
SellPrice:	5.99	
IncomeEarned:	$3,566,092.59	
Income Per Title:	$142,643.70	
RoyaltyRate:	15%	
Total Royalties:	$534,913.89	﹀

4. Add an entry for the new author.

a) In the **Authors** data form, select **New**.

b) Enter the following information in the fields.

Authors	? ✕
AuthorID: **3000**	New Record
InitialContract Date:	**New**
YearsUnder Contract:	Delete
Status: **Active**	Restore
Origin: **New Contract**	Find Prev
Genre: **Sci Fi**	Find Next
Agent Code: **5035**	Criteria
Payment Method: **DD**	
State (if US): **TX**	Close
Country Code: **001**	
Number of Titles in Print:	
Number of Books Sold:	
SellPrice:	
IncomeEarned:	
Income Per Title:	
RoyaltyRate:	
Total Royalties:	

c) Select **Close**.

5. Navigate to the bottom of the worksheet, if necessary, and verify that Excel added the new record.

6. Navigate up to row **13** and verify that the entries for author 1032 have been updated.

	A	B	C	D	E	F	G	H	I	J
1	AuthorID	Initial Contract Date	Years Under Contract	Status	Origin	Genre	Agent Code	Payment Method	State (if US)	Country Code
13	1032	1/6/2007	7.05	Retained	Legacy	Romance	5072	DD	NJ	001

7. Save the workbook.

ACTIVITY I-2
Adding Form Controls

Before You Begin

The My Author Master Roster.xlsx workbook file is open.

Scenario

 Note: The datafile in this activity is incomplete and only reflects the topic working with forms and controls.

As the number of Fuller and Ackerman authors continues to grow, you have decided you want to create a dashboard worksheet so users can easily look up a variety of information about various authors. You know form controls include some functionality that you will find useful as you develop the authors dashboard, so you will begin building the dashboard by adding a combo box that can be used to select any author ID from the **Authors** worksheet.

1. Add the **Developer** tab to the ribbon.
   a) Select **File→Options→Customize Ribbon**.
   b) In the **Customize the Ribbon** list, check the **Developer** check box.

   ☑ View
   ☑ Developer
   ☑ Add-ins

   c) Select **OK**.

2. Change the name of **Sheet2** to *Author_Dashboard*

3. Add labels for the first item in the dashboard.
   a) On the **Author_Dashboard** worksheet, add the label *Look Up Author Income* to cell **A1**.
   b) Add the label *AuthorID* to cell **A3** and the label *Income* to cell **A4**.
   c) Adjust the width of column **A** to accommodate the text.

4. Add a form control to the worksheet.
   a) Select **Developer→Controls→Insert**.

b) In the **Form Controls** section, select **Combo Box (Form Control)**.

c) Drag the mouse pointer to draw the combo box on top of cell **B3**.

> **Note:** Draw the combo box so that it is the same size as cell **B3**.

	A	B	C
1	Look Up Author Income		
2			
3	AuthorID		
4	Income		
5			

5. Configure the combo box properties.

a) With the combo box still selected, select **Developer→Controls→Properties**.

b) In the **Format Control** dialog box, ensure that the **Control** tab is selected.

c) In the **Input range** field, type *AuthorID*

d) In the **Cell link** field, enter *$C$3*

e) Change the value in the **Drop down lines** field to *10* and then select **OK**.

>
> **Note:** Setting the **Drop down lines** field changes the number of displayed values when a user selects the combo box drop-down arrow.

6. Ensure that the combo box works as expected.

> **Note:** The combo box returns the entry (index) reference for the selected ID, which is its numerical place in the column of data.

a) Select any cell on the worksheet other than **B3** to deselect the combo box.

b) Use the combo box's **drop-down arrow** to select **1006** from the drop-down list.

c) Ensure that Excel returns the value **2** in cell **C3**.

	A	B	C	D
1	Look Up Author Income			
2				
3	AuthorID	1006	2	
4	Income			

d) Select cell **C3** and then press **Delete**.

7. Change the combo box cell link so Excel hides the entry reference behind the combo box.

> **Note:** The reason for hiding the returned entry reference is that it acts as a space saver and gives the worksheet a less cluttered appearance.

a) Right-click the combo box and select **Format Control**.

b) Change the entry in the **Cell link** field from **$C$3** to *$B$3* and then select **OK**.

> **Note:** You can make another selection from the combo box to see that the returned entry reference is hidden. Using the keyboard, you can select cell **B3** to delete the returned value.

8. Save the workbook and close the file.

Mastery Builders

Mastery Builders are provided for certain lessons as additional learning resources for this course. Mastery Builders are developed for selected lessons within a course in cases when they seem most instructionally useful as well as technically feasible. In general, Mastery Builders are supplemental, optional unguided practice and may or may not be performed as part of the classroom activities. Your instructor will consider setup requirements, classroom timing, and instructional needs to determine which Mastery Builders are appropriate for you to perform, and at what point during the class. If you do not perform the Mastery Builders in class, your instructor can tell you if you can perform them independently as self-study, and if there are any special setup requirements.

Mastery Builder 1–1
Working with Multiple Worksheets and Workbooks

Activity Time: 15 minutes

Data Files

C:\091057Data\Working with Multiple Worksheets and Workbooks\Total Sales.xlsx

C:\091057Data\Working with Multiple Worksheets and Workbooks\Quarterly Sales.xlsx

C:\091057Data\Working with Multiple Worksheets and Workbooks\Pricing.xlsx

Scenario

As sales manager for Develetech Industries, you have been tracking the quantity sold for each of the product lines. You have already entered all the sales figures for the first three quarters of the year and now need to calculate the total sales for the fourth quarter on each of the regional worksheets: NA, Europe, and Asia. You need to create an external 3-D formula to calculate the sales for each product by multiplying quantity and price. Once this is complete, you need to consolidate the total sales data on the Product Sales Totals worksheet.

---

1. Navigate to the **C:\091057Data\Working with Multiple Worksheets and Workbooks** folder. Open the workbooks **Total Sales.xlsx**, **Quarterly Sales.xlsx**, and **Pricing.xlsx**.

2. Create an external 3-D formula to multiply price from **Pricing.xlsx** and quantity sold from **Quarterly Sales.xlsx** for each of the regional worksheets, **NA**, **Europe**, and **Asia** for the fourth quarter of each of the worksheets in **Total Sales.xlsx**.

3. Consolidate the sales data from **NA**, **Europe**, and **Asia** on the **Product Sales Totals** worksheet using the **SUM** function.

Mastery Builder 2-1
Using Lookup Functions and Formula Auditing

Activity Time: 10 minutes

Data File

C:\091057Data\Using Lookup Functions and Formula Auditing\Sales Commission.xlsx

Scenario

As the sales manager for Develetech Industries, you have been tracking the progress of your sales people. You have created a workbook that contains two worksheets, one to track the salespersons earnings for each quarter and another for the commission rate scale. You want to look up the commission rate for each salesperson based on the rounded sales figures. Next, you want to check your workbook for errors in any formula or function.

---

1. Navigate to **C:\091057Data\Using Lookup Functions and Formula Auditing** and open the **Sales Commission.xlsx** workbook.

2. Create a Lookup function to calculate the commission rate for each salesperson from the named range **CommScale** in the range **H4:H7**.

3. Trace precedents for the new Commission Rate Lookup function and remove the arrows.

4. Trace precedents for the total sales range **B9:F9** and remove the arrows.

5. Find any errors in the workbook and show the calculation steps evaluating the function.

6. Edit the error in the **Formula Bar**.

Mastery Builder 3-1
Sharing and Protecting Workbooks

Activity Time: 10 minutes

Data File

C:\091057Data\Sharing and Protecting Workbooks\Expenses.xlsx

Scenario

Working in the accounting department, you have created an expense workbook. This workbook tracks the travel expenses for several salespersons each month. You want to protect the workbook from being edited so you decide to protect the formulas you created and the workbook from being modified. You also mark the workbook as final, indicating that you have completed editing the file through December.

1. Navigate to the **C:\091057Data\Sharing and Protecting Workbooks** folder and open the **Expenses.xlsx** workbook.

2. Save the file as *My Expenses.xlsx*

3. Hide the total sales calculations on the monthly expense worksheets but allow users to select the cells and protect each worksheet.

4. Protect the workbook from additional changes and add the password *password*.

5. Mark the workbook as final.

6. Close the file.

Mastery Builder 4–1
Automating Workbook Functionality

Activity Time: 15 minutes

Data File

C:\091057Data\Automating Workbook Functionality\Expenses.xlsx

Scenario

You need to create a worksheet with a listing of expenses being recorded for several salespersons. Rather than repeating the same process on each worksheet, you decide to automate the task by creating a macro that will record your actions of creating the expense sheets.

1. Navigate to the **C:\091057Data\Automating Workbook Functionality** folder and open **Expenses.xlsx**.

2. Starting from the **October** worksheet, record a macro named **ExpenseSheet** that sets up the content on new expense worksheets and include the shortcut key **Ctrl+Shift+E**.

3. Enter and format the following information in the worksheet:
   - Format cell **A1** bold and increase the font size to 14.
   - In cell **A4**, type *Auto Rental.*
   - In cell **A5**, type *Air Fare.*
   - In cell **A6**, type *Lodging.*
   - In cell **A7**, type *Food/Meals.*
   - In cell **A8**, type *Parking.*
   - In cell **A9**, type *Total.*
   - Format the range **A4:A9** bold.
   - In cell **B3**, type *Lyons.*
   - In cell **C3**, type *Norris.*
   - In cell **D3**, type *Lloyd.*
   - In cell **E3**, type *Banks.*
   - Format the range **B3:E3** bold and underline.
   - Format the range **B4:E9** with currency number format.
   - Enter a formula in the Total row that calculates the total expenses for each person.

4. Stop recording the macro.

5. Run the **ExpenseSheet** macro on the **November** worksheet.

6. Edit the macro to remove the underline format from the range **B3:E3**.

7. Run the updated macro on all the worksheets in the workbook.

8. Save the file as a macro-enabled workbook named *My Expenses.xlsm* and close the workbook.

Mastery Builder 5-1
Creating Sparklines and Mapping Data

Activity Time: 15 minutes

Data Files

C:\091057Data\Creating Sparklines and Mapping Data\Euro Sales.xlsx

C:\091057Data\Creating Sparklines and Mapping Data\Tornado Data.xlsx

Scenario

You have been tracking European sales in a spreadsheet to present to management. While you could easily create a chart to display all the European sales data, you think it would make the chart difficult to read so you decide to create sparklines for the year-to-date data. In another file you have been asked to show the progression of the reports of tornadoes and their strength in the United States from 2013. You decide the best way to show this is with a 3D Map.

---

1. Navigate to the **C:\091057Data\Creating Sparklines and Mapping Data** folder and open the **Euro Sales.xlsx** file.

2. Save the file as *My Euro Sales.xlsx*

3. Create YTD line sparklines for each of the European countries in **F2:F21**.

4. Show the high and low point markers on the line sparklines.

5. Save the file and close the **My Euro Sales.xlsx** workbook.

6. Navigate to the **C:\091057Data\Creating Sparklines and Mapping Data** folder and open the **Tornado Data.xlsx** file.

7. Save the file as *My Tornado Data.xlsx*

8. Create a 3D Map from the Tornado Data table.
   a) Select the **Heat Map** visualization.
   b) Set **Location** to **Begin_Latitude**.
   c) Set **Value** to **F_Scale**.
   d) Set **Time** to **Begin_Date**.
   e) Hide the **Field List**.
   f) Adjust the Layer 1 legend as necessary.
   g) Adjust the map as necessary.
   h) Play the scene.

9. Close 3D Maps.

10. Save and close the file.

Mastery Builder 6-1
Forecasting Data

Activity Time: 15 minutes

Data File

C:\091057Data\Forecasting Data\Projections.xlsx

Scenario

You are working on various sales projections for your company. You have a file containing three worksheets that you need to create projections for future data. On the Budget worksheet, you have been asked to see how the projected budgets would change by varying the interest rate for the budget increase. On the Vendors worksheet, you want to see three scenarios by changing the percentage increases for two years and to see the impact on the projected sales. On the NW Sales worksheet, you have collected monthly sales data and want to forecast sales in the future.

1. Navigate to the **C:\091057Data\Forecasting Data** folder and open the **Projections.xlsx** file.

2. Save the file as *My Projections.xlsx*

3. On the **Budget** worksheet, starting with the range **D6:D7**, AutoFill down to cell **D16** to input a column of percentages from 5% to 10%.

4. Use a formula in cell **E5** to reference the formula in cell **B3**.

5. Create a one-input data table in the range **D5:E16**.

6. On the **Vendors** worksheet, create a *Normal Sales* scenario using **B4** and **B6** as the changing cells and then create two additional scenarios.
   - Best Case: **B4**=.15; **B6**=.1
   - Worst Case: **B4**=.05; **B6**=.03

7. Show each scenario and create a **Scenario Summary** using cells **B3**, **B5**, and **B7** as result cells.

8. On the **NW Sales** worksheet, create a **Forecast Sheet** to the forecast end of **3/15/2017**.

9. Save the file and close the workbook.

Glossary

3-D references
References to the same cell across a range of worksheets.

ActiveX controls
Type of control that is far more flexible and customizable than form controls. ActiveX controls can execute VBA code authored by users or developers.

calculated columns
In Power Pivot, columns populated by aggregating data with the use of Data Analysis Expression (DAX) formulas.

change tracking
Excel feature that adds page markup to workbook changes, making it easy for users to identify revisions.

comments
A type of worksheet markup that allows workbook users to convey information to one another.

control properties
Control settings that assign specific functionality to controls, configure visual formatting options, define the linked cells, and determine how controls interact with the associated worksheet.

controls
Objects that users can add to worksheets that help other users perform certain tasks, such as entering data.

data consolidation
The process of summarizing data from a variety of datasets that aren't necessarily laid out in the same fashion.

Data Model
In Power Pivot, the relationships among various tables imported into the corresponding workbook that enable users to make meaningful queries based on data in the various tables.

data tables
Excel what-if analysis tool that enables users to replace one value in one or more formulas or functions, or replace two values in a single formula or function to determine a set of possible outcomes.

data validation
Excel feature that enables users to restrict data entry to particular specified criteria.

dependent cells
Cells that are fed by the data in other cells.

Developer tab
Ribbon tab that users can add to the Excel ribbon in order to access the commands and tools for adding new functionality to Excel.

Excel Online
Web-based version of Excel that is used for collaborating on documents via the Internet. Excel Online does not support all Excel functionality.

external links
Links to cells in other workbooks.

external references
References in formulas or functions to cells in other workbooks.

forecasting
The process of using the trends that exist within past data to predict future outcomes.

form
Either a physical or an electronic document that is organized for the purpose of collecting information.

form controls
Controls that add functionality to Excel worksheets without the need for writing VBA code.

formula evaluation
The process of breaking down Excel formulas or functions into component parts to determine how Excel is performing calculations.

internal links
Links to cells within the same workbook.

invalid data
Data entries that do not conform to the data validation criteria applied to a cell or range.

iterative calculations
Repetitive mathematical operations that approach the approximate solution to a problem by using the output of the previous calculation as part of the input for the subsequent calculation.

linked cells
Cells that are connected to the data in other cells. The data in a linked cell appears as the original data and behaves much like a standard data entry. The data in linked cells updates when the original data is updated.

macro
A series of steps or instructions that users can execute by using a single command or action.

metadata
Data about other data. In Excel, metadata can exist within workbook files and can include such information as the person who last worked on a workbook, the workbook's file size, and the date it was last revised.

modules
Containers for storing VBA code.

one-variable data tables
Type of data table that replaces only a single variable in a formula or function. Users can determine possible outcomes for multiple formulas or functions by using one-variable data tables.

personal workbook
Hidden Excel workbook that users can use to store macros for use in other workbooks.

precedent cells
Cells that feed data into other cells.

scenarios
A type of what-if analysis that enables you to define multiple variables for multiple formulas or functions to determine a variety of outcomes.

shared workbook
An Excel workbook with certain collaboration features enabled. Shared workbooks enable multiple users to contribute changes to a workbook file that can then be merged together in the master copy of the workbook.

sparklines
Data visualization tools that exist within worksheet cells and display the relative values of entries in the defined dataset.

tour

A 3D Map time-based relationship between geographic locations and their associated data.

trace arrows

Worksheet markup that visually identifies relationships among worksheet cells.

two-variable data tables

Type of data table that replaces two variables in a formula or function to determine a range of possible outcomes.

vector

A data range that consists of either a single row or a single column of populated cells.

Visual Basic Editor

Development tool used for creating and editing VBA code.

Visual Basic for Applications

The programming language that developers use for Microsoft Office applications and other related add-ins, macros, and applications.

Watch Window

Excel feature that enables users to view the contents of specified cells regardless of their location on a worksheet.

what-if analysis

The process of calculating possible outcomes by replacing particular formula or function values with a set of variables.

Index